Also by Michael W. Clune

White Out: The Secret Life of Heroin
Writing Against Time
American Literature and the Free Market

Gamelife

Farrar, Straus and Giroux
New York

Gamelife

A Memoir

Michael W. Clune

For Jenny and Sean

Farrar, Straus and Giroux
18 West 18th Street, New York 10011

Printed in the United States of America
First edition, 2015

Library of Congress Cataloging-in-Publication Data
Clune, Michael W.
    Gamelife : a memoir / Michael Clune. — First edition.
        pages   cm
    ISBN 978-0-86547-828-2 (hardcover) — ISBN 978-0-374-71317-1 (e-book)
    1. Clune, Michael W.—Childhood and youth.   2. Computer games—
History.   3. Video games—History.   4. Video gamers—United States—
Biography.   I. Title.

GV1469.15 .C59 2015
794.8—dc23

                                                                    2015004993

Designed by Jonathan D. Lippincott

Contents

Gamelife

1.

Suspended

I wasn't surprised when the computer appeared. I'd seen it coming on TV. Television was pictures on a screen. After television came the words. In the den of our old Victorian house in Evanston, after the VCR tape of *The Parent Trap* was over and my sister Jenny dozed beside me, and my parents were upstairs and hadn't yet noticed the television babble had stopped, I watched the static. I waited for something to emerge. I was seven. After fifteen minutes, nothing. After twenty minutes, still nothing. After a half hour the static was like a pulverized alphabet. Ten minutes later I saw the first letter. W. Assembled in a flash from tiny gray and black slats, it jumped from one corner of the screen to the other and vanished.

So I was ready for the words at the end of television. My father set up the computer in the small second-floor room by the back staircase. My mother said that in the old days that had been the nursery. She said my great-grandfather had lived in that room when he was a baby. He was dead, I'd never met him. My mother said he was probably thinking about me.

The Commodore 64 was a swollen beige keyboard. The small television and the keyboard housing the mysterious computer circuits sat on a card table. I sat on a wooden chair—an extra from the kitchen table far below. Behind the ex–television screen, and slightly above it, a narrow window showed the blue summer sky. The pre-words of high clouds spun in the static of the sun. I realized why the default setting of the computer screen is blue. I typed in a sentence.

-Color 2

The screen changed to green.

-Color 3

The screen changed to red.

-Color 10

-ERROR

-Color 15

-ERROR

-Make Castle

-ERROR

The first thing a human needs to know about computers is that not every sequence of words will work. The second thing a human needs to know about computers is that almost every sequence of words will not work. I took a deep breath. I looked down at the keyboard, a hive of unknown words. XFK. CRYSTEP. SEPT1HLP. Which combinations would work? Which ones were error?

I stared at the red screen. The undersides of my legs grew sweaty on the hard wood chair.

-Make

I stopped typing. The cursor blinked at me. Make what? I closed my eyes. Nothing. The error was in me! I didn't know what I wanted from the computer.

When my father found me, he gently raised my head from the keyboard. He dried my eyes with the edge of his shirt. Then he started to tell me about computer games. A computer game is a device for giving people things to want from computers.

The game I picked out with my father at the store was called *Suspended*. It belonged to a now-forgotten genre known as "text-based adventures." It was made by a company called Infocom, which had practically invented the genre with their 1978 game *Zork*. The front of the box had a picture. On the back of the box were words:

A robot who hears but cannot see . . .

You are suspended—physically immobilized, frozen but alive—20 miles beneath the surface of an automated planet. Three computers, supposedly perfect and fail-safe, control the entire planet's weather, transportation, and food production. You are linked to the computer system in case of an emergency—in case, for some unthinkable, unimaginable reason, the computers malfunction.

A robot who sees but cannot wander . . .

Should the impossible happen, should something go wrong, you must fix the computers as quickly as possible, since people will be dying—victims of a utopia turned nightmare—unless you do.

A robot who feels but cannot hear . . .

You cannot move. You have six robots at your disposal to do your work for you—highly specialized, programmed robots, all obedient, all helpful, all individualized. You will have to manipulate them in and around an Underground Complex where the computers are controlled. You will address and work them separately and jointly, and they will report back to you with their progress and perceptions.

Think logically. Act decisively.

This description mesmerized me. I read it through four times. Then I turned the box over to examine the picture on the front. A man's large blue face. His eyes closed. Suspended, I thought.

"How old are you, son?"

I jumped a little. It was a clerk, staring down at me through wire-rim glasses.

"Um . . . seven," I stammered.

He shook his head.

"This game is designed for older players," he said. "Ages sixteen and up."

He took the box from me and replaced it on the shelf.

"There's some games you might like over in the next aisle," he said. "Fun games."

I turned where he pointed and walked away, dazed. Sixteen? I did the math in my head. From seven to sixteen is . . . nine. Nine years until I would be sixteen. I couldn't wait nine years!

I stopped. The aisle was piled with brightly colored boxes. I looked at them. Games about mazes. Baseball. There was even a box with Big Bird on the cover. No way. I turned around. Leaned past a shelf piled with computer manuals to scan the aisle I'd just left. The clerk had his back to me, talking to another customer. I inched back toward the *Suspended* boxes.

What if I got it anyway?

I looked over my shoulder, suddenly worried that my father was watching. But he was at the counter, chatting with the cashier. So what if I play it nine years early? I thought. It's a game. How could it be dangerous?

I'm going to get it, I decided. I crept up and snatched the box from the shelf, and walked as quickly as my legs would carry me to the counter.

Hurry, I thought, looking back for the bad clerk.

My father glanced at the box, nodded. I gave it to the cashier so he could ring it up. The cashier looked at me, but he didn't say anything.

My father had the radio on as we drove back from the store. President Reagan was on it. He was talking about Iran. He said that the best gift human beings could give to the future was an error-free world.

"We will not stand for error," Reagan intoned.

"Eliminate error," my father whispered to himself.

No more error, I thought. Outside the car windows, the giant summer daisies turned slowly on their stems. The road beneath us vibrated like an eyeless, earless, noseless robot. Deep summer blue above, the color of swarming airplanes.

Everything is about to change, I thought.

•

"You have been awakened."

Floppy disk inserted, computer turned on, a whirring, and then this sentence, followed by a blinking cursor. I'd lowered the blinds over the window, but the rims of sunwheels slid through the slats.

I studied the card with the list of words the game recognized. It was a short list. "Report." "Move." "Press Button."

"Auda, report," I typed.

Auda was the robot who could hear.

"I hear wind coming from the sloping corridor."

I studied the colored map that had come with the game.

"Iris, report," I typed.

Iris was the seeing robot.

"I am in the Transit Control Area. The screen shows malfunctioning aircabs have now killed twelve thousand people on the surface. There are three buttons."

"Iris, press button."

"I do not have hands," she said.

"Sensa here," scrolled across the screen. "I am picking up a disturbance by elevator bank A."

"Auda, report," I typed.

"I am hearing the sound of footsteps in the sloping corridor," she said.

"Whiz, report."

Whiz had intelligence.

"I am in the data library sir. What would you like to know?"

"What are the footsteps?"

"I don't know what that means."

"Iris here. Malfunctioning aircabs have now killed twenty thousand people on the surface. There are three buttons."

"Auda, press button," I typed.

"There is no button here," she said.

"Sensa here," scrolled across the screen. "I am sensing a disturbance in the library."

I checked the colored map. The sloping corridor led from the elevator banks to the library.

"Whiz, report," I typed.

"Whiz has been disabled," scrolled across the screen.

"Auda, move to Transit Control Area," I typed.

"I don't know what that is," Auda replied.

I studied the command sheet, studied the map.

"Auda, move southeast," I typed.

"Moving southeast," she said.

"You hear footsteps in the room outside your chamber," the screen scrolled. "You see shadowy shapes bent over the controls of your cryogenic suspension tank. Your life support systems have been disabled. You have failed."

The screen went black.

"What the hell?" I said.

After a few seconds the frustration drained away, and it hit me: I'd been inside. I'd been *somewhere else*. I looked to see where it was I was.

An angle of sunlight cut across the reflection of the small boy in the computer screen. Summer wind moved behind the walls. The boy's great-grandfather stood behind the wooden chair. He stood without eyes, without ears, without hands.

•

The next time I played, I discovered Waldo, a robot with multiple arms who could move quickly and lift heavy things. Waldo, Iris, Auda, Sensa, Whiz, and Poet. Poet could sense the flow of electricity. I also discovered the hulk of a seventh robot. I moved Waldo to the Transit Control Area, where he was able to operate the controls that disabled the aircabs, which ended the murder on the planet's surface and delayed the arrival of the squad sent to disable me.

I also discovered a strange text on the back of the game manual, after the page with the commands. It was a paragraph long, and it described the game's creator. His name was Michael Berlyn. The paragraph described how Michael was a valued and creative member of the Infocom team. It said that he drank a great deal of coffee. It then said that he had worked too hard on *Suspended*, and that he had become insane following completion of the game. At the time, I didn't understand that this was game-designer humor.

"Do you know anyone who has become insane?" I asked James.

James was my cousin from Ireland, visiting for the summer. He was three years older than me and had wonderful fair hair, and all the girls in our summer school class had a crush on him. We were sitting on the beach a couple of blocks from my house. James shrugged.

"Me mother went insane," he said. "From drugs, it was."

I was taken aback.

"She's okay now, though?"

I'd seen my aunt just last summer. A large, warm, melancholy woman.

"Oh, ay, she's right enough now," said James.

"So . . . when you become insane, do—"

"Why are you so fascinated with becoming insane all of a sudden?" James asked.

"I'm not," I said. "So when you become insane, what happens?"

He shrugged.

"I dunno."

"But you said your mother—"

"Look," he said. "Now I'm going to tell you just this one thing and then we're going to shut up about insanity, all right?"

I nodded.

"Right then," he said. "When you get insane, you can't talk right."

"Can't talk right. Like how?"

An idea occurred to me.

"Like you don't understand a lot of sentences?"

He nodded.

"What else?"

"Your hearing gets messed. Like I'll be after talking to her for ten minutes and it'll be like she heard nothin'."

I was astounded. James noticed.

"Can she move her hands?" I breathed.

"You mean when she's insane?" He thought about it. "Yes," he said. "I mean no."

He looked over his shoulder. My little sister, Jenny, who we were supposed to be keeping an eye on, was making drip castles by the water.

"I'll tell you something else, if you keep it quiet," he said.

It was getting late. The sun's giant face was crossed with air transit lines, and on the lawns behind the beach, the daisies had stopped moving. The lake droned.

"Insane people see things that aren't there," James whispered.

"Oh!" I said.

"And it's inside," he said. "It's inside that it goes bad. When you're insane, it's the inside that rots. The things she'd say, her not understanding plain English, the look in her eyes. Well that's all small stuff, really. But it's what it *shows* that counts. What it shows about what's happening inside."

"What's happening inside?"

"It was the priest told us that," James said. "The priest said *her soul is disturbed*."

"Poet, touch seventh robot," I typed.

"I am detecting faint electrical activity within this hulk," Poet said.

"Iris, look at seventh robot."

"I see a giant robot. Its eyes are closed."

"Sensa, report."

"I sense a disturbance inside the seventh robot."

"Auda, what do you hear?"

"I don't understand that."

"Auda, listen to the robot."

"I don't understand that."

"Auda, report."

"I hear wind," said Auda. "I hear footsteps."

•

"I wish I could stay here," said James.

"You have to go back to Ireland at the end of the summer," my little sister told him. "You have to go back to school."

"Shut up, Jenny."

"Everybody has to go back to school."

"Jenny, you be quiet," my mother called from the front of the station wagon.

We were on our way to Studio M. Mrs. Larson, the third-grade teacher from St. Mary's, the small Catholic school Jenny and I attended, ran a month-long summer session of creative activities for gifted children. The criteria for giftedness were elastic. Jenny's gift, for example, was complaining that if James and I got to go, then she should be able to go. My gift was lip-synching. James's gift was writing.

The low brick school building pulsed dully in the sun. We trooped out of the station wagon. I was the last to leave, and as I got out, my mother reached through the car's open window to grab my shirt.

"Michael," she hissed.

"What, Mom?"

"Shhhh!"

She looked furtively at the school entrance twenty paces away, where James and Jenny stared back at us. She pulled me close.

"James can't stay with us," she hissed in my ear.

"What?"

"He's going to want to, and honey, I wish we could. God knows, he's going to want to stay with us even more now that his mother—damn it!"

Jenny was running toward the car.

"What, Mom?" I asked.

"Nothing!" she called out, loud enough for James to hear. "Have a good time, children. See you in two hours!"

The station wagon sped off into the summer haze.

"What was she on about?" James asked.

"Who knows?" I said.

Inside, we joined the seven other gifted members of Studio M. Mrs. Larson stood over everyone, beaming. She was a hyperactive woman gifted at projecting her facial expressions through time and space using the funnels of children's brains. What Mrs. Larson expressed was happiness. Her face worked exclusively with happiness. Compacted into impossible densities in the pressures of her interior, concentrated happiness sprang out of her face, uncoiling through our spiral lives.

When her expression of joy emerges at the other end of us it will be a constellation in the sky.

I love her.

"Who wants to start?" she sang delightedly.

"Start what, Mrs. Larson?" we chorused.

"With a creative event!" She sprang to the blackboard, yellow chalk stick in hand.

"In the last week who has experienced a CREATIVE EVENT?"

And as our answers babbled out she answered herself, shouting, "Everyone! Everyone has experienced a creative event. Neil!"

"I finished *Prince Caspian*," said Neil, a blond kid whose

father worked for the FBI and had a gun. *"Prince Caspian* is one of the *Chronicles of Narnia."*

"Wonderful, Neil!" said Mrs. Larson, the magic words of the title unspooling from her pinwheeling hand at the board. "A wonderful book! To read a book is to create! Without a reader the words are just marks! They're nothing!"

"Errors!" I shouted.

"Yes, Michael!" she screamed. "Yes, exactly! A book by itself is an error! A reader like Neil is a CREATOR! James!"

"I started writing a story, Mrs. Larson."

She had to sit down. She pulled up one of the tiny chairs meant for eight-year-olds and lowered herself onto it. We leaned forward.

"Now maybe," she whispered, "maybe your wonderful Irish accent has tricked my poor old ears, James. But I thought you said . . . no! You can't have. You can't have started . . . started to write . . ."

She looked at him imploringly.

"I've started a story, Mrs. Larson."

Looking directly up at God, she ascended from her chair like the space shuttle.

"But a story without a reader is nothing," Neil called out worriedly. "Reading is the creative part! Like *Prince Caspian.* Right, Mrs. Larson?"

"To write is to commune with the unborn," she said, "Tell us about the story, James."

"Me story's called 'Firefox,' " he said.

"*My* story," she corrected.

"*My* story," he continued. "It's about a bad computer that comes through the power lines, like, to electrocute people."

"That's amazing," she said. "Tell me more."

"That's all I've got, like. This wicked computer that'll come through the wires and blow up yer telly."

"And then what?" asked Elizabeth, a dark-haired girl I was in love with.

"Whaddaya mean?" James said. "And so it blows up yer telly and then ya call the FBI and they pull out all the wires and they follow it to the computer and they shut it down and ya buy a new telly and *it happens again.*"

Joy poured out of Mrs. Larson's face.

"It happens again," she breathed. "Every moment is unique. Every instant is singular. And *it happens again.* The secret of creation. It happens again and again and again. Listen! Do you know what the word 'omnipresent' means, children?"

We shook our heads.

"It means the Holy Spirit is everywhere," she said. The quiet joy had come suddenly into her face. "And children, you might have something happen. Something like what happened in James's story. Something rare and magical. And you might say to yourself, This cannot happen again. What are the chances? you might say. Once in a lifetime. Have you heard your parents say that, children? Have you heard them speak of a *once-in-a-lifetime event*?"

We nodded, thinking of Disney World.

"Well," she said. "Let me tell you a secret, children. The *once-in-a-lifetime event* happens again. It happens again and again. Let me share something wonderful with you."

She clasped her hands, the loud joy climbing back into her eyes.

"If I had a dollar for every once-in-a-lifetime event," she sang, "if I had a dollar for every impossible, incredible, never-to-be-repeated event that will happen to every single one of you children! For example, if I had a dollar for every once-in-a-lifetime event that will happen to *you*, Elizabeth . . . do you know how many dollars I would have?"

Elizabeth shook her head.

"Five *trillion*," said Mrs. Larson. "*Five* trillion. *Five trillion*."

•

"Iris, report."

"Malfunctioning aircabs have now killed twenty thousand people on the surface. There are three buttons."

"Waldo, press middle button."

"I have pressed the middle button."

"Iris, report."

"Aircab activity has now halted."

"Poet, move south."

"I am now in the Outer Library."

"Poet, move south."

"I am now in the Index Peripheral."

"Poet, move south."

"I am now in the Central Core."

"Poet, report."

"I detect massive watts of energy moving in knots behind the panels."

The knots were words, I knew.

"Whiz, report."

"I am in the Central Core."

"Use."

"Use what?"

"Use knots."

"I don't know what that means."

"Read."

"Read what?"

"Read energy knots."

"I don't know what that means."

"You hear footsteps in the room outside your chamber,"

the screen scrolled. "You see shadowy shapes bent over the controls of your cryogenic suspension tank. Your life support systems have been disabled. You have failed."

•

"How many times can you die?" I asked James.

"Three," he said. "You mean in *Pac-Man*?"

"No, in life," I said.

"Oh," he said. He thought. "I don't think you can die too many times."

"How many?" I persisted.

"Well," he said. "Jesus. Now, come on with yourself."

"What?"

"Well, how many stories have you heard where someone dies, and then they die *again*?"

"In *Suspended* I die every day," I whispered.

"What?"

"*Suspended*," I said. "In *Suspended* I die all the time."

"Whaddaya mean, you die all the time? How many?"

"I don't know."

"Look, Michael," he said. "If ya had to venture a guess about how many fuckin' times you can die in fuckin' *Suspended*, what would you say?"

His swearing made me anxious.

"I don't know!" I said. "A trillion."

His eyes widened. "A *trillion*, is it?"

"If I had to guess," I said. "Yes. One trillion times."

He seemed impressed. He looked down at his feet, the way he did when he was thinking about something secret. The way he did after his father called on the phone from Ireland. Finally, he shook his head.

"Listen to us two fools! *Suspended* is only a game. Sure,

how many lives you've got in *Suspended* doesn't mean anything more than how many lives you've got in *Pac-Man*."

"It's nothing like *Pac-Man*," I said hotly. "Pac-Man's not
even a person."

"And *Suspended* is only robots! You told me yerself."

"There's more than robots," I said. "You don't know what
you're talking about, James. *Suspended* has a person in it."

"Oh yeah, who?"

"Me!" I said. "I am. I'm a person in *Suspended*."

"But come on now," James lectured me. "You can't move or
touch or see or hear or anything in *Suspended*. You need a robot
to do everything for you. I don't call that being a person."

"That doesn't mean I'm not a person," I said.

"Yes it does," he said.

That night I imagined myself lying on my bed. Then I took
away my hands. Okay, I thought, now I can't feel the bedsheet.
But I'm still a person. Then I took away my mouth. I can't talk
now, I'm still a person. Then I imagined my ears closing in on
themselves like flowers at night. No sounds, but I'm still a person. I took away my eyes. Now I couldn't see myself lying there.
I couldn't feel myself in the bed. I couldn't hear anything.

I'm a person, I thought. I am a person who can die one trillion times.

•

James never played *Suspended* with me. After dinner, James
and Jenny and my mom would gather before the big TV down-
stairs where the Atari was plugged in and play *Pac-Man* or
Donkey Kong while I climbed the back stairs to the computer
room alone. James never came.

"To be honest with you, Michael," he said to me one evening at dinner, "that game sounds boring as hell. I don't want to play it. And to be perfectly honest, I don't want to hear about that fucking game again."

"James!" said my mother, shocked.

"Sorry, Auntie Barb," James said, looking into his potatoes.

My sister smiled at me. My mother placed her knife and fork on her plate.

"James," she said, "you might be able to say those words at home in Ireland. But you are not at home now."

"Yes, Auntie Barb," he said.

"This isn't your home," she said. "This isn't *like* your home in Ireland."

"All right, Barb," said my father, swallowing his last mouthful and pushing back his plate.

"I'm just saying," said my mother. "Jenny and Michael are here."

"All right," my father said.

That night I made my great breakthrough in *Suspended*. I'd been trying to get Whiz to tell me what was in the library data banks. I knew it would help me. I'd gone as far as I could on my own. I stopped the aircabs from killing people. But the planet's other systems, the air and water and food systems I was responsible for, they were too complicated.

I now knew that I had only six turns after each new success before the footsteps of the mysterious strangers came to shut me down. I needed another success. I needed a hint, a clue.

The answer, I believed, lay in deciphering the obscure fate of my *predecessor*. I learned of this shadowy figure by accident. I had been moving Poet through the underground complex to the Hydroponics Control Center, but I must have gotten lost. When I asked for his report he said: "I am in the room with the seventh robot. The one your predecessor disabled."

"Who is my predecessor?" I typed with trembling hands.

"I don't know what that means."

"What is predecessor?"

"I don't know what that means."

Whiz, I thought. Whiz could tell me. The fifth robot possessed enormous intelligence, and once I'd moved him to the library, he had access to the accumulated knowledge of an entire planet. But I didn't know the command that would unlock it.

That night, after the dinner where my mother had twice reminded James that our home was not like his home, I found the correct command.

"Whiz, tell me about predecessor."

"I don't know what that means."

"Speak to me about predecessor."

"I don't know what that means."

"Communicate to me about predecessor."

"I don't know what that means."

I got desperate: "Pray to me about predecessor."

And then I let go and fell into the darkness:

"Whiz, know to me about predecessor."

"Understand to me about predecessor."

"Make predecessor known to me."

"Press button of word, predecessor."

"Tell me about predecessor, please."

"Open predecessor word."

"Use word. Predecessor."

I searched my brains for the correct command. And then the breakthrough. This is the breakthrough: When you meet the thing that lives outside of nature, do not look inside your own head to discover what to say.

Look in the book.

Look in the card with the list of words. The card that came with the game.

Methodically, I typed every word on the list before the word "predecessor" and pressed enter. It was the first methodical thing I had done in my life.

No one remembers the first time they saw their mother. No one remembers the moment they first recognized that the thing in the mirror is *me*. But the generation of humans who were approximately seven years old when PC games first became widely available, we remember the first time we did something methodical.

"*Drop* predecessor."

"I don't know what that means."

"*Enter* predecessor."

"I don't know what that means."

"*Exit* predecessor."

"I don't know what that means."

"*Find* predecessor."

"I don't know what that means."

"*Go* predecessor."

"I don't know what that means."

Look at card, look at keyboard, type word on card on keyboard. When you have gotten to the bottom of your senses and your capacity to think, you are ready to embrace method. To embrace method is to become the pure servant of fate.

One of Goya's Black Paintings depicts a vast thickening shapeless yellowy mass. At the very bottom left corner, a few daubs of brown and black paint depict the head of a tiny dog. The dog's senses twitch baffled at the edge of the mottled yellowish endless stuff of the world. It is a picture of the animal getting to the bottom of its senses. It is a picture of the basic animal experience of wonder.

A human is a dog with *method*.

"*Halt* predecessor."

"*Hit* predecessor."

"*Join* predecessor."

"*Kill* predecessor."

"*Lift* predecessor."

Look at card, look at keyboard, type word on card on keyboard. Method. A wheel made out of simple repetitive movements. It wears through the rock of the world like a river.

"*Query* predecessor."

It was the last word on the sheet. I typed it and pressed enter.

"Your predecessor," said Whiz, "was removed for gross incompetence. He caused millions of deaths on the surface. His cryogenic suspension life support apparatus was disabled. His life was terminated."

Trembling, I typed: "Query removed."

"Your predecessor was removed because he became insane," Whiz reported.

·

"If I just had another week," James said, "I could finish 'Firefox.'"

He'd covered dozens of pages in the notebook Mrs. Larson had given him.

"And I could finish *Suspended*," I said.

He looked at me sharply.

"Are you nuts?" he said. "*You're* not the one has to leave here and go back to fuckin' Ireland."

We were at the beach. In the distance, by the water, Jenny dripped wet sand into piles until it made wet sandpiles. That's how it is in this world.

"What happens next in 'Firefox'?" I asked, to pacify him.

"The computer, it's after strangling people up with the cords of their own telephones," he said, looking into the white sky. "And so the agents, like, they've all resolved to do without telephones and tellies and anything electric. And now one is after looking at the other and he says, All right, Agent Red, Firefox can't get at us."

"But," I broke in, "but then the agents can't get to Firefox. It *works* through telephones and TVs. It is *in* them."

"Exactly!" James said. "Fucking *exactly*, Michael. It can't get to us but, like, how in Jesus' holy fucking name are we to get to it?"

"Without the things it works through, Firefox is, it's like a television without . . ."

I stopped and we stared at each other.

"It's like a telly without a telly," James finished.

"What's left of a telephone," I said softly, "after you take away the telephone?"

"Not nothing," he said. "Firefox is still there."

"Oh I know," I said. "It's still there. It's worse, even. Now it's *everywhere*."

"I wish I had another week," he said, pounding his fist into the sand. "I could finish it if I had another week."

"I really wish you would play *Suspended*," I said. "It says it's for ages sixteen and over and you're three years closer to sixteen than me and we could play it together and then we'd be, like, seventeen and . . ."

But he was shaking his head.

"That game's driving you mad," he said.

The sky had gone flat white and the sounds of the birds had died. Jenny dripped wet sand onto wet sand.

"Michael," he began. "Where I live in Ireland, like. It's not the way it is here where you live."

"What do you mean?" I asked.

"Never mind," he said.

He turned to look at the lake, and I stared at him. Sometimes when he wasn't looking I stared at him. If James is here, I thought, and then he goes away, then what's left of him?

Not nothing, I thought. Not nothing. Not nothing.

I shivered. The sky was a flat white sheet.

•

By the time we got home, the sky had thickened, turned yellowish, mottled. My mother was on the steps, her tiny face tilted up to the gigantic sky.

"There's a tornado watch," she said distractedly.

"A tornado!" said Jenny.

"A tornado is nothing to be happy about," my mother said severely. "It destroys houses."

Jenny smiled at her. I was terrified.

"Shouldn't we go to the basement?" I asked.

My mother shook her head.

"It's just a tornado *watch* for now," she said. "If it becomes a tornado *warning* the sirens will go off and then we'll have to go to the basement."

"But what if there's not enough time?"

"Go to the den and watch TV."

It was so dark outside when we got to the den that when James turned his head away from the TV beam to speak to me, darkness erased his features.

"What?" he asked.

"I said, D-d-don't you think we should turn the v-v-volume on the TV down," I stammered.

The television threw its pictures one after another into my brain, where they melted.

"Are you pulling me leg, Michael?" James said.

"He's scared of the tornado," said Jenny. "He's scared he won't be able to hear the siren."

James laughed.

"But how will ye hear the tornado siren, Michael," he said, "with all the other sirens?"

Then he cupped his hands to his mouth and began to imitate the high whine of a police siren.

"Weee-ooo-weee-ooo-weee-ooo."

Jenny clapped her hands and joined in.

"Weee-ooooo."

"Shut up!" I shouted. "Stop it!"

Behind their braying imitations, I could hear the true whine starting. The thin serrated alien voice of the tornado siren. It came into the house and cut through their voices like a whipsaw through chicken meat.

"Jesus," James said. "Listen."

Jenny's small voice now harmonized with the siren. Her face took on the wan and serious look she'd had when singing in the first-grade Christmas concert.

"Weeee-oooo-weeee-oooo-weeee-oooo."

"Shut it, Jenny," James grunted. "Yer ma's calling us."

"Down to the basement!"

My mother stood at the stairs shouting up to us. We ran down the staircase. I imagined the tornado dropping its trunk through the roof like an elephant and drinking the staircase up in a swirl of wood chips.

We huddled in the basement under a naked lightbulb. My mother had a small radio and Harry Caray's voice announcing the Cubs game came through whirling chips of static.

"They'll say on the radio if the tornado's coming," my mother said.

"Jesus," James whispered.

"James!" My mother yelled.

But he wasn't swearing. He was praying. His lips pressed into a pale wavering line, his face bone white in the stark light. His hand reached out and grabbed mine, squeezing tightly.

"It's going to be okay," I managed to whisper.

"It *destroys houses*," he said through gritted teeth.

"Be quiet!" said my mother.

I squeezed James's hand tightly. Harry Caray spoke out of the radio, heartless.

"And it's still the top of the eighth, and there's still only one out, and, folks, if these Chicago Cubs have ever needed divine intervention, boy, I am here to tell you it is today, folks."

Thunder spoke through the bones of the house.

"Don't let go of me hand," James whispered.

"I won't," I whispered.

•

The tornado uncoiled harmlessly into the air it was made of. The warning expired after a half hour. The Cubs lost. James left for Ireland a week later. The next time I saw him, four years had passed. My family was visiting my grandmother in Ireland and he came into the kitchen where we were all drinking tea and talking. He had changed.

When he was leaving, I said I had to go to the bathroom and ran out and caught him in the hall and asked him. What about "Firefox"? Oh, that silly thing, he said. But what about the notebook, I said. You still have the notebook. Oh, I don't know what happened to it, he said. Me mammy probably tossed it. He left.

I wanted him to ask me about *Suspended*. What about *Suspended*? How did it end? What happened with the seventh robot?

I don't know, I would have told him. I never finished it either. Just like you with "Firefox."

But it wasn't just like him. "Firefox" was gone in the way of being completely gone, but *Suspended* was gone in the way of being everywhere. It was my first computer game. I played it at the right time. I don't know what would have happened if I had waited until I was sixteen, but playing it at seven changed me. It gave me a new direction to grow. While my parents and friends and teachers were helping part of me to grow up toward the people, another part of me had begun to grow out, away from them.

2.

Four Hundred and Ninety Points of Damage

It isn't easy to grow away from the people. You need imagination. My imagination was as weak as a baby's arm until computer games trained it. I can't even remember the things I imagined before computer games. Giant Legos, maybe? Flying dogs? People's faces? When I was eleven, computer games taught me how to imagine something so it lasts, so it *feels real*.

The secret is numbers. Imagination fumbles outside reality like a child at a locked door. The key is numbers. In 1986 I discovered *The Bard's Tale II*. It was the first computer game I ever played that was derived from *Dungeons & Dragons*. *D&D* was created in 1974 by Gary Gygax, who had discovered the secret to making imaginary worlds real. *Dungeons & Dragons* adds numbers to fantasy.

When you play *Dungeons & Dragons* and your character attacks a giant wolf, you roll the dice to see whether the blade connects with wolf flesh. You roll the dice again to determine the extent of the damage dealt. The Dungeon Master rolls the dice to see if you will encounter a giant wolf in the first place. And every aspect of your character—his strength, his dexterity, his intelligence—is composed of the numbers revealed

by the dice. *D&D* is a fantasy world governed by numbers.
Numbers add the flavor of reality to fantasy. Roll the dice. 22:
You encounter a giant wolf. 17: You fail to cast the spell *fireball*. 14: The wolf's bite severs your leg. You're not just making this up, read the dice. 3: You successfully cast the spell
fireball and the wolf burns into a shadow on the cave's wall.

Gygax brought numbers into fantasy. But every force for
good is also and equally a force for evil. There is a dark side
to *D&D*. This darkness has two dimensions. The first is
moral and the second is practical.

The first problem is that at around age one, a healthy
human being discovers the world is made of words and delights in this. That's a dog. That's a Lego. The Lego is under
the table. At approximately age one, the human child feels the
power of words awaken within him. He delights to discover
that the world responds to his words. When he calls to the
world in words, the world hears and answers. The dog comes.
The Lego is a Lego. The child rejoices to know that the world
is made of the same wordstuff as his new mind.

But actually he's wrong and the world is made of numbers.

Actually the child is dead wrong and words belong to the
people but nature or the alien thing we call nature or God is
made entirely out of numbers. If we talk to nature or God in
words, it doesn't understand us. Words just sound like noise
to nature. Science has proved this. Science has shown that
humans live in this world but it isn't for us. We can use numbers but numbers are not our natural language, and when we
use numbers we are borrowing them from someone or something else.

Probably numbers belong to the devil. Almost certainly
they do.

This dark truth constantly leaks from the dice of *D&D*.
People in the eighties made fun of the evangelical Christian

groups who wanted to ban *D&D*, but I don't think you have to be an evangelical Christian to know that there is such a thing as an evil truth and to know that it leaks constantly from the fantasy of numbers.

That's the moral drawback to Gygax's creation. The practical drawback to *D&D* was that I couldn't get anyone to play it with me.

"That shit is for hyper nerds," said Eric, mashing buttons on his Sega controller. His quarterback threw a ninety-yard pass over the heads of my defenders.

"Forty-eight to nothing," he sang.

Sega games, Nintendo games, PlayStation games, Xbox games, Wii games. Unlike PC games, video games will always be with us. They require actual hand-eye coordination. Like the real sports they resemble and are often about, video games have a place in social reality. But they lack contact with the reality beneath society.

"I think my controller is broken," I said.

"Is that number on Eric's side a 48?" asked Rich, Eric's preternaturally intelligent little brother.

"Shut up, Rich," I snapped.

"I mean," Rich asked, "is that, I mean is that a zero on Mike's side?"

"Why does your little brother have to hang out with us?" I asked Eric.

But Eric was looking at Rich.

"Yeah, it's a zero, Rich. Mike's losing again. So what?"

"Is it okay if I bring Mike to my science class?" Rich asked.

Eric threw back his curly, athletic head and laughed.

"Shut the hell up, Rich," I said.

Rich jumped up and stood in front of the TV screen, pointing at the numbers.

"No, I'm serious," he said. "Look—48 and Mike has zero.

Last game it was 64 and Mike has zero. Before that it was 71 and Mike has zero."

Eric laughed. Rich jumped up and down.

"Eric! Eric! Can I please bring Mike to my science class?"

"Why do you want to bring him to your science class, Rich?" Eric asked, grinning.

"I can't say!"

"Why can't you say?"

An anxious eager serious look sprang out of Rich's face.

"I can't say, because it's a bad word," he said. "I mean, it's a real natural thing and it's a good thing 'cause it's natural, but I can't say it because the only word I know for it is a bad word. Can I bring Mike to my science class, please?"

"Shut the fuck up, Rich," I said. "Eric, why the hell does Rich have to hang out with us?"

Rich was squirming around before the television screen like he had to piss. "I want to say it!"

"What's the word, Rich?" Eric asked him. "What's the word for what Mike has?"

I hit Eric on the bicep.

"Mom will get mad if I say!" Rich whispered.

"Say it," Eric said, laughing, wriggling easily out of my attempt to get him in a headlock.

"It's a natural thing!" Rich yelled. "It's not a bad thing!"

"Say it, Rich," Eric demanded. "Say it, Rich, or I'ma beat your ass."

Rich looked furtively down the hallway.

"*Retarded*," he whispered.

I got up.

"It's not a bad thing!" he yelled. "It's a natural thing! Forty-eight to zero, 64 to zero! It's a scientific thing! Mike's retarded!"

I pushed him to the ground. Rich waited until I had sat

down again. Then he leaped up, incandescent in the television light. His little body shook with anger. He pointed at me.

"*You* can't push me," he said through tiny gritted teeth. "*You* can't tell me I can't take you to my science class. *You* can't do anything. *You* are *retarded* and my science teacher said that *retarded* people CANNOT decide by themselves what to do or where to go and that means you CANNOT decide whether you will come to my science class or not!"

"Your little brother creeps me out," I told Eric.

"Me too," he said.

Eric wasn't laughing anymore. Rich stood in the center of the room vibrating at a thousand times per second. His mouth was open and his teeth looked like broken bits of television.

"Time for your nap, Rich," Eric said uneasily.

"No!" Rich said. Numbers writhed under his tongue.

Eric turned off the TV and hit the lights, and it was a little better. Then he picked up a shoe and hit Rich across the face with it, and Rich ran off crying and we were alone.

"You do suck at Sega football, though," Eric said.

"I want to play *D&D*," I said. "Come on! I know where to buy a book and dice."

"It's for dorks," Eric said. "Everyone at school would make fun of us. Everyone on the basketball team. Elizabeth would break up with me."

"No one will know," I told him.

Eric was a fun, healthy kid. He had a broad, open face and a tall, strong body. He was constantly laughing with his wonderful laugh that rinsed whatever was laughed at in sun. When Tim fell off the top of the tornado slide and broke his neck, Eric laughed. It was a laugh without malice. Eric laughed a laugh that loved the bright surfaces of the world. He laughed out of pure, thoughtless devotion to noise and color. Especially if he saw something new, he'd laugh. He couldn't help it. He even laughed at an aluminum baseball bat the first time he saw one. I was there, I saw it.

Eric's laugh was spiritual and it wasn't at all what the counselor said after Tim got hurt. That shock sometimes makes people laugh when they feel like crying. The counselor said it in a dark way that implied that anyone who laughed at someone breaking their neck because they felt like laughing was infected with devils. But I knew that Eric was maybe the one person in America who could laugh at someone who'd just broken his neck and do it from pure spiritual joy. Tim didn't die from the fall, and I don't know about him, but for myself I can say that if the last sound I hear when I do die is Eric laughing at me, I will consider the sound to be appropriate and even holy.

But Eric's brothers were different.

"My brother Henry plays *Dungeons & Dragons*," Eric said finally.

Many years older than Eric and me, Henry lived in the attic. He was far into high school. I didn't know how far. Far enough to drive a car by himself. And Henry was bad. Something was wrong with him. Even my mom said so. No one ever told us how he was bad, but everyone knew he was. So when Eric said that Henry played *D&D*, I understood that it was his final word on the matter and that nothing would ever convince him to try it.

But one Saturday later that fall, while Eric was being lectured to in the kitchen by his harried single-parent mother, I crept up the attic stairs. Henry's door was ajar. I could hear Eric's mother's voice from far below like a dozen frantic chickens, gobbling up the spaces left by Eric's inaudible replies.

I drew my breath in slowly. I put my foot to the back of each step, where the creak was mildest.

Three steps from the top, I heard a sound coming from

Henry's room. It was a sound like rain on a tiny dome. A small, circumscribed clatter.

I crouched down on the landing and put my head through the door.

The sound got louder. Rain on a miniature glass dome.

Henry's back was to me. The dark curls of the bloodline he shared with Eric spilled down the back of a dirty Christmas sweater. White, with green and red clocks on it. He sat before a long wooden table. Another kid sat next to him. A bad kid. Hunched over the table, greasy blond hair spilling down a green sweater with red Christmas trees.

The sound of my fast breathing. The sound of my fast breathing and the sound of rain on the windows of a tiny dark town. Clatter. Clatter. Clatter.

And every five seconds Henry's right arm jerked back behind him. His right arm jerked back behind him and released a sound like the clatter of rain on a tiny dome.

And then through the opening he made when he raised his arm, I saw the scarlet flash of *red dice with white numbers*. And then a hand gripped the back of my neck and I spun around, opening my mouth to scream and Eric's other hand shot over my mouth, his pupils like the heads of black nails, and Henry's voice now booming out over us:

"Hey, you kids like to watch us play? You twerps like to sneak and watch us play? You *fucking* little rats like to sneak up and watch us roll these *fucking* dice?"

Booming out over us as we raced down the stairs passing Eric's mom going slowly up with an ashen face, not even seeing us, hands clutched, intoning, "Now, Henry, calm down. Calm down now, Henry, calm down. Calm down, calm down."

And that Sunday in church, my father did what he always did. While the priest droned out the words of God, my father leaned down and directed my attention to the wood panel with five rows of three-digit numbers beside the altar. Every pew had a thick hymnbook, and the numbers referred to the hymns that were to be sung at that morning's service. But my father, though he sang dutifully with everyone else, was interested in the numbers for themselves.

"If you can memorize those," he whispered. "There's five dollars for you, Michael."

He'd quiz me a few hours after the service, and if he saw I'd written the numbers down I'd get nothing. I had to commit them to memory. There were words all over the church, but my father never asked me to memorize those. He wanted to improve my memory and the hymn numbers were tougher than the Bible phrases. He saw nothing sacrilegious in what he was doing. He saw no spiritual significance in the fact that numbers are harder to memorize than words. He saw no warning in the fact that a child's soft brain resists numbers. That the neural tissue swells up around a number like the soft skin of the thumb swells up around a splinter, pushing it out.

For one hour every week of my life, I stared at numbers while words to and about God rose and fell around me. I stared at numbers during the reading of the New Testament. I stared at numbers through incense clouds when the deacon swung the censer. I even stared at the numbers while walking slowly back from Communion, head bowed, the Eucharist dissolving in my mouth.

"We will now turn to hymn number 490."

I bought *The Bard's Tale II* with the money I earned from memorizing numbers in church.

•

The illustrations on the *The Bard's Tale II* box left no doubt that it contained a computerized *Dungeons & Dragons*. For one thing, there was a large circular picture of a dragon menacing a party of adventurers on the front. For another, the picture was surrounded by hundreds of tiny black *runes* on a gray faux-stone background. Runes are druidic hieroglyphs. They resemble bent and burnt G's, Y's, and X's. Runes are letters, frozen in the process of turning into numbers. They are the universal symbol of total fantasy.

I had to buy it. It was the only way. The practical problem with *Dungeons & Dragons* was that you had to find friends to play it with. And even if you had such friends, there was still the basic paradox of fantasy games. The basic paradox is that the very power of a fantasy fused with numbers saps your ability to maintain the social relationships that are the scaffolding that supports the game. Enraptured by the gameworld, you find it hard to remember or care about the qualities that made the people sitting around the table your friends in the first place. Eventually you lose them.

Eventually Henry would roll his scarlet dice alone.

But unlike *D&D*, *The Bard's Tale II* was designed to be played alone. Even if I had been able to find some perfect friend to play it with me who would never stop being my *Dungeons & Dragons* friend, no matter how much we grew to loathe each other in real life, *The Bard's Tale II* was still better. Instead of some kid pretending to be the Dungeon Master, the fathomless computer was the dungeon master. And instead of rolling dice to determine the outcome of a giant wolf attack or a fireball spell, you pressed a key and the computer generated a random number.

I had never played a game like this. Technically, the name of the genre that *The Bard's Tale II* was an early example of is "computer role-playing games" (CRPG). But this name is highly misleading, because every game—from *Pac-Man* to *Super Mario Brothers* to *Call of Duty*—places the player in a "role." You play as Pac-Man, as Mario, or as some World War II soldier.

The genre "role-playing game" is even more misleading if you think that games in the genre will have particularly fascinating roles for the player to play. As if the genre appealed primarily to the theater-club crowd.

"How did you get your start, Christian Bale?"

The actor strokes his chin.

"I guess it all started with computer role-playing games," he says. "Then I started acting in movies."

The truth is that the role you play in a role-playing game is as unimportant as the role you play in *Pac-Man*. In *Pac-Man*, you play a yellow circular being who loves dots and fears ghosts. In computer role-playing games, you play a medieval adventurer who loves weapons and fears dragons.

The role is not important. What is important is the thing you see through the hole of the role. The genre should really be called: "The cave where the Numbers become flesh." I inserted the floppy disk and turned on the computer. The machine whizzed, the television bristled with static, then smoothed out blackly. The title—*The Bard's Tale II: The Destiny Knight*— scrolled across the screen. I hit enter and the blinking icon hovering over "Start New Game" froze, the screen went blank, and the new game started.

The first part of every computer role-playing game is "character creation." This is where you type in the name of your character and press the button and the game uses random numbers to create a person. My character, whom I named Eric, began the game with 8 hit points. That's the amount of damage he could take before dying. Eric had a dagger that did 5 points of damage with every successful strike. He had a dexterity of 16—which meant he had about a 50 percent chance of landing a successful strike—and a leather shield that had a 75 percent chance of protecting him from 4 points of damage.

Eric was a fighter. That's a description of his profession. In the same character creation sequence where I created Eric, I also created five other characters. A wizard, an archer, a thief, and two other fighters. Together, they were me. We were I. I pressed enter and the world began.

I—we—were on a grassy field of breathtaking beauty. A forest surrounded us.

W moved us forward. A turned us left. D turned us right.

We turned around on the field. The picture of the grassy field took up the upper left quarter of the television screen the computer plugged into. The bottom half of the screen was filled with the statistics of my party—hit points, armor points, spell points, current weapons. The upper right quarter was currently blank, but would soon be filled with the statistics of the enemy forces we faced, the scrolling numeric readout of the battles, and various verbal messages the game had for us.

The upper left corner was what I saw. The upper right corner was what I knew. The bottom half was what I was made of.

It took me a few hours to get used to this new body. But after that, my soul never chafed in it. All you really need for a good body is something that sees, something that knows, and some numbers underneath. I have spent more hours in computer role-playing game bodies than some people who have recently learned how to walk and how to tie their shoes have spent in human bodies.

So I know how to walk and how to tie my shoes in the cave where Numbers become flesh.

As we stared in wonder at the pure green of the grass, a

group of five goblins made out of giant gray pixels approached
and attacked us. Battle! First it was their turn.

—Goblin strikes Eric and *misses*.

—Goblin strikes Eric and *misses*.

—Goblin strikes Eric and *hits* for 7 damage, leather shield
blocks 4.

—Goblin fires an arrow at Jenny and *misses*.

Then it was our turn. Eric's name was blinking. I looked at
the game manual. I pressed [space] to have Eric attack with
his current weapon.

—Eric strikes goblin and *hits* for 8 points of damage. One
goblin dies.

A small quantity of VICTORY dripped into my bloodstream. I jerked in my chair, grinning nervously. It was a new
feeling for me. At age eleven you haven't had many opportu-
nities to triumph over your enemies. After the next goblin went
down, I felt it again. Wow. Soon I got used to it.

After a couple hours I learned that my new body was capable of three feelings: VICTORY, DEFEAT, and FRUSTRA-
TION. This might seem like too few to you who can also feel
ENVY, BOREDOM, FEAR, and LOVE. But if you have seen
black-and-white movies, you know that only two colors can do
a pretty good job of making a decent world. Similarly, if you're
having three feelings hard and often, you don't really miss the
other four. My little party used daggers, hunting bows, and
magic missiles to turn the goblins' numbers into nothing.

We wandered around killing a few giant wolves, a few
more goblins, and a party of dark elves. VICTORY ticked in
my heart. I found a helmet on one of the dark elves and put it on
Eric and his armor points went up. Now Eric had a 75 percent
chance of blocking 6 points of damage. We were growing
stronger. VICTORY is not just fun. It actually makes you stron-

ger. I looked at the shiny laminated map that came with the game, and we headed persistently east through the forest. In the forest we had a tough battle with some orcs, but it ended in a red bath of VICTORY. Eric and James had now accumulated enough battle experience to move up a level. That meant I got to press [space] and the computer rolled its dice and Eric got six more hit points and James got eight.

I felt we were ready for more dangerous monsters. The map indicated great evil to the east. East of the forest rose the walls of a city. Just outside the city we encountered the long, green, shapeless mass of a troll. It attacked.

—Troll strikes Eric and *hits* for 490 damage. Eric dies.

—Troll strikes James and *hits* for 462 damage. James dies.

—Troll strikes Jenny and *hits* for 512 damage. Jenny dies.

My veins ran black with DEFEAT.

DEFEAT enters the bloodstream in a fine black dust of pulverized numbers. It is unpleasant. It is in fact more toxic than death, which is after all temporary, and can be immediately erased by pressing the enter key upon dying, thus loading the game from the last time you saved your progress. Multiple deaths in rapid succession, however, bring the real risk of FRUSTRATION.

FRUSTRATION is the slow expansion of a zero in the artery of the computer role-playing game body. Zero—the empty number, round gate leading from the fantasy of numbers to the world of numberless people. Further deaths in rapid succession will cause the zero to swell and to swell until it gets large enough for the rhythms of a *human body* to be felt inside the game body.

The stiffness of my spine in the hard wooden chair. The pressure in my bladder.

When the zero gets large enough, swollen with dozens and

dozens of deaths, you can actually see your human hands on the keyboard. You can see the thick late December sun pushing through the slats of the blinds. And now an alien feeling, BOREDOM, beats in the very numbers of the game.

The true death is almost here, and now through the zero of FRUSTRATION you experience the FEAR of the true death.

If, however, at its widest point, the zero of FRUSTRA-TION is lanced by VICTORY, then the spiky rune of VIC-TORY gets pushed up your veins through the pleasure-giving membranes of a collapsed zero. It enters the heart like a comet.

•

Why does fantasy with numbers *work* and *last* and *move* when fantasy without numbers *sits* and *dribbles* and *whines*? Think about ordinary, numberless fantasy. There is nothing more natural and human than fantasy. The baby sits in its diaper fantasizing a breast. The phantom breast is the baby's first experience of its natural ability to create something that is not there. Human flesh is the quarry of worlds. The baby already has enough flesh to create a fantasy mother. Look! There it is. The baby's natural response to its act of creation is to cry.

So much for unaided fantasy.

But what does it take for the baby to drink from the fantasy breast?

What does it take for the human to take up residence in the world of fantasy? To breathe unreal air? Walk on unreal ground? Eat unreal apples?

We find clues in the way the human being breathes real air, walks on real ground, eats real apples. The human depends on the inhuman. The human depends on the inhuman for its grip on the world. Inside every human face that crumples in sudden sorrow is a skull that grins. Unfeeling bone supports every hug. The ancient, primitive mollusk suction-and-release of our orifices gives our words breath and makes our thoughts go. Human feeling *leans* on the inhuman. Human feeling advances into the world leaning on the stick of inhumanity.

So if you want to move into the world of fantasy, you need the support of the inhuman. Something in or under your fantasy that is not you, that is not like you, that does not like you. The addition and subtraction of numbers. The multiplication and division of numbers. Put the rule of numbers in your fantasy like a spine of bone and you will walk out into what is not there. Let addition and subtraction be the suction-and-release of your fantasy body and you will breathe unreality and speak magic. Lean on the rule of numbers like a cane of bone and you will shuffle out of space and time.

I will tell you what it feels like to be immortal.

The past is full of VICTORY. The present is full of numbers. The future is full of VICTORY.

Some people might say that this game immortality isn't real immortality. They might say game immortality is just mortality's weak fantasy. You die and live again in the game, okay, they might say. But then you get up from your chair, the power goes out, the phone rings, morning comes, you fall asleep and fall out of the game and you're the same mortal human as everyone else. You don't stay in the game. You can't stay in the game. You can't die forever in the game, but because you can't stay in the game forever you can die forever. Game immortality isn't genuine immortality.

Except it is. You can be immortal for a little while. Every religion and every myth system and every folklore tradition contains examples of beings who were immortal and became mortal, or who were mortal and became immortal. Think of Jesus or Arwen. This doesn't prove that myth or religion are right, of course. Religion doesn't prove that temporary immortality is possible. It just proves that the *idea* of temporary immortality isn't nonsensical. *The Bard's Tale II* proves that temporary habitation of an immortal body is possible.

I learned all this within a month of getting *The Bard's Tale II*. These were things that my parents' generation never learned at all. Yet I experienced the primary feelings of an immortal before I experienced sexual feelings. It frightened my mother to death.

"What is this?" she breathed.

She was in the computer room at the top of the back stairs, turning *The Bard's Tale II* box over in her hand.

"What are you doing up here, Mom?" I asked.

She whipped around to face me. Cheekbones burned bright in her white cheeks. "Where did you get this?"

She raised the box between thumb and forefinger.

"What?" I was baffled. "At the store. I mean, I didn't steal it or anything. Dad gives me money at church for memorizing the numbers you can ask him I—"

"*What is this.*"

She held it out to me. I scanned the box anxiously, looking for something maybe I'd somehow missed. A swear word? Tits? But there was just the picture of the dragon, the inoffensive title, and the runic decor.

"It's *The Bard's Tale II*, Mom," I stammered. "You, like, go around this world and you have a sword, um, a dagger really for now, but you can find swords, it says in the manual."

She wasn't listening.

"Does your father know about this?"

"Dad?"

She placed the box on the computer table, then turned to me, hands on hips. I noticed, stupidly, that her long, curly hair was the same length and color and texture as Henry's.

"Now, Michael," she said quietly. "I want you to put everything that came in this box *back* into the box. I want you to do it right now."

I couldn't believe what was happening.

"What! Why?"

She pressed her lips together until the color ran out and her lips looked like the thin side of a steel dagger.

"This game is evil," she hissed. "Put it back in the box now and give it to me."

Frustration and defeat boiled in my throat as I packed the game up under her savage eye. Fear churned in my stomach and lower, in my lowest gut, the deadly liquid of boredom was already moving. My computer role-playing game–less life stretched out before me: seventy years of sports and sports-based video games ending in a death that was final.

That evening, when my father stepped in the door knocking snow from his boots and smiling, my mother thrust the box in his face.

"Did you know your son had this?"

"Give me a minute to get in the door, Barb. Jeez."

Jenny was jumping up to try to see the box and my mother was twisting around, simultaneously trying to show it to Dad and shield it from Jenny.

"Look at it!"

He took it and studied it, turned over the back, and returned it, mystified.

"Is it s-e-x?" he spelled, looking nervously at me.

"No!" Mom shouted. "It's *Dungeons & Dragons*! Oprah

had a show on this. It's turning kids into satanists. They're acting out the violence from it in school!"

"Mom," I said, appalled by these fantastic lies, "come on, it's just a game!"

"And I just got off the phone with Ellen," she went on. "Her son Henry's life has been *ruined* by *Dungeons & Dragons*! He didn't even *apply* to college and God knows what will become of him when he graduates. Ellen says he's even applied for a job at the *post office*."

"There's always room for satanists at the post office," my father said, smiling down at Jenny.

"This is serious," my mother wailed. "I want you right now to take a look at this writing around the edge here. Here, right by the picture."

My father took the box and began to study the runes closely.

"What the hell is it," he said to himself. "It's not letters . . . no, these aren't any kind of letters I've ever seen. This looks like a six crossed with a . . . ."

"*A six crossed with a Y*," my mother whispered. "The whole box is covered with these things. Jenny, go into the other room."

"What does it mean?" my father said, serious now and looking at me. "Who gave this to you?"

"It's just," I said weakly, "it's just like some kind of old-fashioned writing it doesn't mean anything it's a game."

I had a horrible feeling inside.

"Well, I don't think this game is a good idea for you," said my father flatly.

My mother sighed with relief.

"Good," she said. "I'll hide it."

"It's *my game*," I yelled. "I *bought* it. I *love* it. I want it *back*."

"He's like a cult member," said my mother. "Look. He can't help himself."

"I want to know what store would sell something like that to a kid," my father said.

"Look at him," said my mother with fear in her voice.

She looks at me. Her vision is wind moving in a field of numbers. Her fear is a number stuck headfirst into mortal flesh.

•

My mother was serious about hiding the game. That weekend, when she and my father went out to a fund-raiser, I opened every closed drawer in the house and looked under every bed. I found the plastic Uzi she'd taken away from me when I was nine and the black Michael Jackson jacket she'd taken away from me the same year after she had a bad dream about it. But I couldn't find *The Bard's Tale II*.

"Here," my mother said the next day, handing me a box. "I got this for you. It's a nice game. It's called *Where in the World Is Carmen Sandiego?*"

Carmen Sandiego was a word game. No hit points. No armor points. No calculation of probability. My desire for *The Bard's Tale II* grew stronger. I resorted to desperate measures.

One afternoon, Eric and I were at the gym waiting for basketball practice to start and playing cards—hearts, the only game we really knew how to play.

"You like hearts?" I asked.

"Sure," he said.

"So do I."

We continued playing.

"Hey, Eric."

"What?"

"What do you call this?"

"It's the king of hearts," he said. "Duh."

"Looks like he's holding something. Here."

"Yeah," Eric said, peering at the card. "Against his chest. Some kind of sword or something. I never noticed that before."

"I bet you could stab someone pretty good with a sword like that."

"Yeah," said Eric. He laughed.

"You know," I said. "When a player picks up the king of hearts, you know how they get a point and how it's bad to get points?"

"Yeah," he said cautiously.

"Well, I guess you could say that the king of hearts is kind of *stabbing* the guy who picks it up."

"I guess," he said.

"Well, that's what happens," I said. "And you know what else?"

"What. I mean, hey! There. I win again. Play again?"

"Okay, sure, but you know what else?"

"What?"

"Even though there's no pictures of swords on the other hearts," I said, "They've got them anyway. Because that's what happens. They stab you for a point when you pick them up."

"What about if you shoot the moon?"

"That's not the point. The point is that the heart cards *stand for* fighters with, like, swords. And we're the players, so we're *using* the soldiers to, you know, kill each other."

"Your turn."

"Hold on! Are you listening?"

"Yeah I'm listening."

"So you agree," I said carefully. "You agree that the cards are like fighters? Like fighters with swords?"

"Yeah, fine," he said. "Now take your turn."

"But don't you see what that means?" I said.

"What are you talking about?"

I took a deep breath.

"If you agree that the cards stand for fighters," I said slowly, "and that we're using them to stab each other, then that means that we're basically playing *Dungeons & Dragons*!" I beamed triumphantly at him.

Eric laughed. "You're retarded," he said.

"No, *you're* fucking retarded," I yelled. "You have to be retarded to not see that we're already basically playing *Dungeons & Dragons*. I'll even give you the money to buy the book and the dice if you keep it at your house and we can get Mark to play and—"

"You're spazzing out," Eric said. "I don't want to play cards with a spaz like you."

"*Yes*, you're going to play, bitch," I said, pushing him.

"That's enough," said the coach, walking out of the locker room. "None of that dirty talk in my gym. Clune! Give me ten laps."

•

In the end, deprived of *The Bard's Tale II* itself, I had to pursue its truth indirectly. I made my life into a giant mirror to catch and magnify the sparks emitted from my memories of the game. This happened in phases.

First I began to imagine more. I'd sit on the school bus in the morning and look out the window at the apartment buildings and I could pretend they were ruins, and if it was snowing, I could *see* they were ruins. Inhabited by creatures. Creatures like strangers. And outside the windows of the bus I could see strangers by the dozen and double dozen. Strangers. Enemies.

Orcs. Moving through the snow in enormous jackets. Probably concealing long, serrated bones and maybe even giant deformed mouths under their jackets.

Every day our teachers warned us against strangers; every night our mothers would repeat the phrase *stranger danger*. It was the era of pedophilia hysteria.

"Does Coach look at your privates?"

"What! No!"

"Do you always know when you are being looked at?"

"What are you talking about, Mom?"

"Have you ever felt your skin prickle and turned quickly around and seen a stranger *staring* at you? A stranger in another car, maybe. Maybe another kid, someone staring at you during recess?"

"Yeah." I'd felt that.

"Have you felt that *prickling* with Coach? Have you had the feeling that Coach was *staring* at you?"

"No!"

"Well, just be careful."

She didn't say it, but the prickling feeling I got when people stared at my head was located on my head or my neck. She didn't have to say that the feeling I would get when someone stared at my privates was a prickling feeling in or around my privates.

The strangers moved around aimlessly on the sidewalks as the school bus passed. We all saw them. We all waited nervously for the first prickling sensation in our underwear that would be the sure sign that the strangers had begun to look at our privates. It was even possible that they could be *thinking* of our privates and the prickling feeling would happen. Oh God. I pretended and imagined different ways of killing strangers.

Looking out the window of the bus, I pretended I saw Eric rush up to one of the ruins in the snow. He had a sword now. It was twelve numbers of punishment coiled into tight, bright steel. Jenny raised her bow behind him, covering his advance. I saw the stranger appear on the steps of the ruin and begin to rush down, parting his jacket at the last second to reveal a giant serrated breastbone—a breast *prow*—plunging from his center. It came down on Eric's unprotected thigh for 7 points of damage—Eric had a good armor class but there was always a 25 percent chance of getting hit in an unprotected spot. Jenny's arrow bounced harmlessly off the creature's weaponized breastbone and Eric stabbed his sword in for 12 points of damage. The creature's 10-point neck split and spilled zeros. VICTORY.

But as I sat there on the bus, I didn't feel stronger. Pretend victories didn't feel real. And there was something else. Something from the game I couldn't stop thinking about. Something I'd felt in the game that I couldn't find any way to know or to feel outside it. *What did 490 points of damage feel like?* What would it look like? I could imagine 12 points of damage. A cut-through neck, for instance. A crushed torso. I could even imagine 20 points of damage. A pulverized skull. Both legs sliced cleanly off. But 490 points of damage? Here was a hard limit to my imagination. I simply couldn't imagine up to 490.

I tried to recall the events leading up to the appearance of that terrible number. My mother had taken the game away soon after we'd approached the deadly city of Thessalonica and been slaughtered by the troll.

—Troll strikes Eric and *hits* for 490 damage. Eric dies.

But Eric only had 24 hit points. How many times did 490 go into 24? I don't mean mathematically. I mean, what did it look like? What did it sound like? What did it *feel* like?

And there was something else. If the game had an enemy capable of dealing 490 points of damage, and if the game was designed to enable characters to grow progressively stronger and hardier with accumulated victories, then the only conclusion was that in the future Eric would be able to withstand 490 points of damage and even to deliver 490 points of damage himself. Jesus.

What was this thing that Eric would become? What would his *arm* look like? In my mind the number 490 became Eric's future name. The terrible name of the future Eric. Eventually the smoke from the always burning number 490 came to conceal Eric's features. 490. What kind of eyes would he have? What sword? What legs?

Four hundred ninety points of damage was like a wall at the end of my imagination. I had come to the end of pretending.

•

The breakthrough happened at the real Eric's house. My mom had dropped Jenny and me off to be watched over by Eric's sister, Abigail, who was a freshman in high school. Abigail's life was a device for amplifying the music and image of the pop group Duran Duran.

"*Look* at Simon Le Bon," she said.

Jenny, Rich, Eric, and I stood in her pastel room looking dutifully up at the giant poster of Duran Duran's lead singer. Abigail pointed at the lump of his leather-encased crotch.

"He's got three penises," she whispered.

Eric laughed. I was confused.

"Not really, though," I said.

Abigail looked at me out of the immaculate distance of her teenage eyes.

"Oh yes," she said. She ran a finger over the poster's bulge, which now did seem strangely large to me. "Three."

"Is . . . is that good?" I asked.

"It's wonderful," she breathed. "It's magical."

Eric laughed.

"Abigail knows everything about Simon Le Bon," said Rich seriously. "She has six magazines about him and a book."

I was afraid to ask if Abigail was joking. I felt sure she was joking, and that if I asked, I would be subject once again to the humiliation of having little Rich call me retarded.

But still, some part of me wasn't entirely sure Abigail was joking. *Three penises.* The impossible potency of a triplicate form of life flowered briefly under my eyelids and was gone.

But it was something. A hook. Four hundred ninety points of damage was still a long way off. But the possibility of tripling that which seemed most primally single . . . it was something. Abigail was almost certainly joking. But we advance into the mystery beyond life only by misunderstanding the living.

Abigail turned up the tinny whistle of her Duran Duran–devoted stereo, and first Jenny, then Eric, then I began to turn and step quietly in time to the words rattling around in Simon Le Bon's aluminum throat. Phantom triple penises spun in the air like pinwheels. Rich watched us with open eyes.

"It's too loud," he shouted. "Henry will hear."

Henry, I thought.

"I love you, Simon!" Abigail screamed.

"I love you, Simon," Jenny repeated.

Eric's eyes closed. He stepped rapidly back and forth.

Abigail's breasts moved under her shirt; her mouth opened and moaned under Simon's metal words; red paw prints appeared on her cheeks and neck.

I need to get out of here, I thought.

Jenny began to shake. Eric began to shake. Abigail turned up the music and climbed on her bed and stood trembling with her eyes falling off of her face. I edged toward the door. None of them were looking. Good. I opened the door and slid out, shutting it behind me.

When I got to the stairs leading up to Henry's attic lair, I could hear the clatter of dice. But no voices. *He's alone up there*, I thought. Good.

I crept up the stairs, took a deep breath, and walked up to his open door. His back was to me. Clatter. I saw the red flash of the dice when he released his arm.

"Hey," I said softly.

Henry spun around. An angry red pimple glowed from the center of his forehead; rage darkened his eyes.

"What the hell are you doing in my room, twerp!" he yelled.

Fear gripped my throat, but I managed to say it: "I want to play."

He looked at me scornfully. "Get out of here. Go back down and dance with the others."

He laughed in a deep adult's voice that made me shiver. But he had a fatal weakness. I'd caught him playing *D&D* by himself.

"It's not like you've got anyone *else* to play with," I said.

His laughter vanished.

"I've got people to play with," he muttered. "They're just not around right now."

"Well, *I'm* around right now," I said. "Let's play!"

He stared at me. Duran Duran floated through the open door at my back, sounding weak and toylike in the austere winter light of the attic.

"You don't even have a character," Henry said finally. "You've probably never even played *D&D*. Get out of here."

But I could sense hesitation in his voice.

"I have a character," I said.

"Oh yeah? How many hit points does he have?"

This is my chance, I thought. Say it.

"One thousand two hundred and twelve," I said coldly.

Henry stared at me incredulously.

"You didn't get that number from any dice," he said.

I nodded.

"I don't use dice when I play," I said.

His eyes widened. "You don't use dice?"

"I'll show you," I said. "*I'll* do the numbers."

He laughed derisively. "You? Where are you gonna get the numbers?"

"From *The Bard's Tale II*," I said. "The computer game. You ever heard of computer games?"

Checkmate. I knew Henry didn't have a computer. They only had Sega in that house.

"Course I've heard of computer games," he said defensively.

"Well, I *play* computer games," I said. "And I know *all The Bard's Tale II* numbers. We'll use those numbers. What's your character's name?"

He hesitated.

"Luxor," he said finally.

I nodded. It was a good name. I went and sat at the table. White winter light flashed in the round attic window.

"Wait!" Henry said. "How do I know your numbers are real?"

"Test me."

"Okay," he said. "How much damage does a battle-ax do?"

"What level is the fighter?"

He thought for a moment.

"Fifteen," he said.

"Armor class of the target?"

"Um," he said. "Ten."

"Three hundred damage," I said.

He looked impressed. "That's what it is? Really? In *The Bard's Tale II*?"

"Yes," I said. "Ask me another."

I didn't really know what the number was in *The Bard's Tale II*. I hadn't gotten anywhere close to level fifteen before Mom took the game away. I was making it up. But being there with Henry, it didn't *feel* like I was making it up. It felt like the numbers were beaming directly into my head from *somewhere else*.

"Ask me another," I said.

"Two-handed sword," he said. "Level-twenty fighter."

"Armor class?"

"Ten."

And I knew the answer without thinking. The number leapt shining into my mind.

"Four hundred and ninety points of damage," I said.

I said it slowly. Henry stared at me. And then he nodded. We sat down to play.

It didn't last long. My ignorance of some *D&D* basics soon stirred Henry's suspicions, and before we'd played many turns he kicked me out of his room, telling me never to come back.

But for twenty minutes that afternoon, I was transformed. Luxor swung at a goblin. My character Eric attacked an orc. Henry looked at me, and I spoke out the number that was in me.

Two hundred sixty.

Thirty-two.

Four hundred ninety.

My mind had become a perfect mirror. One by one the numbers looked into it and saw themselves dressed in the skin of a boy.

3.

The Devil in the Garden

The game world exists on flat screens. It is a world of two dimensions. In a computer game, a person's head has two sides. A front and a back. Take *The Bard's Tale II* Eric, for example. One side of him is colored pixels, and the other side is dark.

Heads are different in the real world. In this world, each head has three dimensions. This means that a head is something you can walk all the way around without getting to the end. You might think that three dimensions makes an image more complex and interesting than two dimensions. That's what Michelangelo and Raphael thought. But they're wrong. A 3-D head has many different sides and angles to it, but they're all basically the same. A two-dimensional head, on the other hand, has two genuinely different sides. One side is visible, and the other side is invisible. A 3-D head is visible all the way around. A 3-D head ultimately has only one side.

Let's say you and I were to meet in real life. And let's imagine that while you were admiring my face, you wondered what was on the other side of my head. Well, you could walk right behind my back (I'd let you) and you could see the solid, hairy back of my head. You could stare at it all you wanted to. You could touch it, knock on it even, and when you were done, you could walk back around to the front and look at my face again. My head has no secrets. It's all out in the open, and the dark back side is always only a very short walk away.

But let's say you were to meet *The Bard's Tale II* Eric. And let's say you were to wonder what was on the other side of *his* head. Well, wonder away. You can't see it. The back of his head is not like the front. It differs from the front in a basic way. You might say it differs in a philosophical way. The front of *The Bard's Tale II* Eric's head lies flat on the screen. The back is invisible. So you see that a 2-D head has two genuinely different sides, whereas a 3-D head really has only one side. What you see is what you get with 3-D. With 2-D, you get everything you see, plus everything you can't.

This is what the people behind the craze for 3-D movies and games will never understand. To make a 2-D image 3-D is to kill half of it. It is to murder its better half, the half that accounts for all of its mystery and most of its power. People are not clamoring for more 3-D. Not really. Not if you listen to them. If you listen to them, they'll tell you they get all the 3-D they can handle in the grocery store and the cubicle. They can admire the many sides of their staplers all they want. They can lift and squeeze tomatoes until the store closes. Frankly they're sick of it. That's why they watch so much TV.

I'm not against 3-D. 3-D has its place. It's useful when you're driving, for instance. 3-D is comforting. It's what lets you sink into a couch. It's what lets you get your hand all the way around a doorknob. 3-D is easy. 3-D comes up to you with a smile and an outstretched hand. 3-D is dry land.

2-D is the ocean.

·

The most important head in my eleventh year belongs to
Evan. I met him six months before my twelfth birthday. He
played *Dungeons & Dragons*. I could tell the instant I saw
him. I was the new kid in school. The first semester of my
eleventh year had been spent in the paradise of public school.
Lincoln Middle School. A wonderful, wacky seventies building
in blue, orange, and lime green. It had huge bubble windows
on the first floor. They must have cost a fortune. The whole
building was filled with happiness and color. I got to go there
because Jenny's Catholic school teacher tied her to a chair for
asking to go to the bathroom. My mother had withdrawn both
of us in protest.

I hadn't realized how rich the government was until I got to
public school. The bubble windows were only the beginning.
The teachers drove cars. The library had books. The whole
floor of the gym was made out of the kind of expensive wood
I'd only ever seen in crucifixes.

There was even a computer lab. It was mostly for *Where in
the World Is Carmen Sandiego?* The company that made *Where
in the World Is Carmen Sandiego?* had convinced the government that playing *Where in the World Is Carmen Sandiego?*
would teach kids about life in other countries.

The funny thing is that it's true. Even in the most foreign
countries, they know the basic words from *Where in the
World Is Carmen Sandiego?* "Hello." "Welcome to the Hotel."
"The woman you are looking for is not here." They even have
the same intonation as the foreign characters from *Where in
the World Is Carmen Sandiego?* The same look, the same cheap
sense of mystery. France, Japan, Morocco. If you've played the
game, you know what life in other countries is like.

The shoddiness of the actual world should never be used to
justify shoddy teaching materials. But it's a mark of the wealth

and quality of public education that even the incorporation of *Where in the World Is Carmen Sandiego?* into the curriculum didn't faze me. Sitting in quality seats, walking under quality lighting, surrounded by quality children. The only building that could compare with Lincoln School in its excitement and quality was the airport.

After the fall semester my parents decided they'd over-reacted to Jenny's bondage experience and sent me back to Catholic school. So a few days after New Year's, I stood at the head of the class while Mrs. Boyd introduced me. What was the point? I knew Eric, John, Elizabeth, Peter, and the rest of the dismal crew from my previous years in Catholic school.

But there were a couple of new heads. One of them was Evan's. He sat in the back, supporting his large, flat red face on a super-functional torso. His torso could twist his head at lightning speed so you could never see the back. I soon learned this was a necessary skill for Evan. It was also why he sat in the back of the class. I soon learned that even the nicest girl in there was only waiting for the opportunity to stick an I SUCK BIG DICKS sign on Evan's back. And more than one of the guys wouldn't turn up his nose at the chance to stab Evan in the back of the neck with a pencil.

I stood at the head of the class, transfixed by Evan's face. As with every good Catholic school, there was one chair too few for the number of students, so I stood waiting while Mrs. Boyd left to get an extra chair from the basement storage room. As soon as she left, Evan leaped up and backed into the wall. All the students turned around and yelled.

"Pussy!"

"Fuck that pussy!"

"Look at that pussy's face!"

"Pussy face!"

Peter and John got up and methodically went to work.

Peter—a big black kid—took Evan's left leg while John—an angel-faced Irish kid—grabbed his right arm. Each of them planted a foot on the wall and panted as they tried to pry Evan loose.

"It's like his back's got giant suction cups on it," Peter gasped.

The rest of the class chanted in the background.

"Go! Go! Go! Go!"

Evan was making a kind of snarling sound. He spit on John's shirt. John stopped pulling and slapped Evan hard against the belly.

"Go! Go! Go! Go!"

When Mrs. Boyd came back in, she yelled at everyone to calm down and yelled at Evan and John and Peter to return to their seats.

"You'll give Michael a bad impression of us," she said, smiling down at me.

I could see that she had chosen to go all the way with the absurd charade of introducing me to the school. I'd spent every term but one at St. Mary's since I could walk. It seemed that Mom's bitching about Jenny's abuse had gotten our family marked for special attention. Mrs. Boyd placed the chair she carried at the end of one of the rows, and I sat down. Eric turned around.

"Boyd can't touch you," he whispered. "After what happened with your sister, your whole family's untouchable."

"Yeah," I whispered back.

"You don't even have to whisper," he whispered. "You're untouchable. This year's gonna be awesome."

"This is geography class," Mrs. Boyd announced.

She tapped her pointer at the giant flat map of the world pasted on the front wall.

"Now this is a *flat* map, but the world is *round*," she intoned.

"Who can tell me the difference between the way the *flat* map shows the world, and the way the round world *really* is."

John raised his hand.

"Yes, John."

"Australia isn't there," he said.

"Actually, John," Mrs. Boyd said gently, "Australia is right here."

She tapped it with her pointer.

John shook his head. "That's not Australia."

She bit her lip. *Great*, she was probably thinking. *They've snuck another retard in here. Just my luck, with that Clune kid waiting to run and tell his bitch mom.*

"Oh, I think if we look closely we'll find that this is Australia, John," she said. "See, it's written right here. A-U-S-T-R-A-L-I-A. That spells Australia."

She looked at me and smiled. But John wasn't finished.

"Yeah that's Australia on the *flat* map," he said. "But that's not how Australia looks in the *real world*."

Her smile vanished.

"And just how," she said in a soft warning tone, "do you think Australia looks in the real world, John?"

"I don't *think*," said John. "I *know*. My uncle *lives* in Australia."

Mrs. Boyd stared at him. "That is quite enough out of—"

"Australia looks like a giant penis," John shouted.

"Get out," said Mrs. Boyd.

"That's what my uncle said! He said that Australia looks like a giant cock!"

Mrs. Boyd walked over and grabbed John's shirtfront, pulling him to the door through the students' psychotic laughter.

"You can see it from outer space," John called from the hallway.

When Mrs. Boyd returned, all pretense had gone out of her face.

"What is the difference between the real world and the *map*," she spat.

Elizabeth raised her hand.

"Mountains," she said primly. "A map can't show things like mountains and valleys. Everything's flat on a map."

Mrs. Boyd nodded.

"Yes, Elizabeth," she said. "A map doesn't give us a good sense of terrain features like mountains. Yes. Very good. So that's one difference. What's another difference between the real world and a map? Class? Someone give me another difference."

Silence.

"Evan!"

We all turned around and looked. Evan's shirt had been slightly torn, and his lower lip had puffed up. It gave him a faintly heroic look.

"The difference between a flat map and reality," he said in a monotone. "In a flat map, any way you go, if you go far enough, the world will end."

•

At recess, the rest of the boys went to throw a football around on the snowy field behind the school.

"I'll be there in a sec," I told Eric, who nodded and ran off.

As soon as the bell rang, Evan had run outside and around the corner of the building. He'd kept his back to the wall the whole time, sliding across it like a giant poster, rolling his eyes to watch for sneak attacks. Once Eric had gotten far enough away, I followed Evan's path, furtively checking over my shoulder from time to time to make sure John or Eric wasn't looking.

When I turned the corner, Evan was right there.

"I knew it was you," he said.

"Hey, I'm Mike," I said, sticking out my hand.

He didn't take it.

"I know who you are," he said. "I'm Evan."

He smiled then.

His entire face unfolded into an enormous red smile. Evan's smile irradiated the midwinter gloom. It shone faintly on the gray bricks of the school building.

It was the fakest smile I'd ever seen.

"Stop doing that!" I yelled.

He folded the smile up into a pulsing red point.

"I came here to be by myself," he said.

"Do you play *D&D*?" I asked.

He looked at me ironically. His lips twitched. Miles of anti-social fakery flexed behind them.

"Why does Michael want to know?"

A bolt of anger shot through me. Only adults called me Michael.

"My name is *Mike*."

The smile twitched behind his lips. I took a deep breath. If he really did play *D&D*, I needed him more than he needed me.

"I need someone to play with," I said.

He folded his arms and contemplated me.

"We have a full group," he said finally.

"What do you mean, a full group?"

"A full group. There isn't room for another player. Besides"—he looked with distaste at my ears, my shoes. "I don't think the others would like you."

This was too much.

"Oh yeah, *the others*," I said. " 'Cause you're so popular. What a bunch of bullshit."

I turned around in disgust and began to walk off.

"Wait," he called.

I stopped and looked back.

"You can come over to my house if you want," he said.

Then, incredibly, he smiled. The please-kick-my-teeth-out smile. He lit up the dingy alley with it. I couldn't believe what I was seeing.

"Are you fucking with me?"

"No," he said. "You can come over to my house, if you want. You can come today, if you want. After school. I won't play *D&D* with you. But I have a computer. And we can play *Ultima III* on it."

"Okay," I said.

When the bell rang and we went inside, I asked Mrs. Boyd if I could use the phone to call my mother. She blanched.

"What's wrong, Michael? What happened out there at recess?"

"Nothing," I said.

"You didn't . . . see anything, did you, child?"

I looked down at my shoes.

"Can I please use the phone to call my mother, Mrs. Boyd?"

"Certainly, Michael, certainly! Come with me!"

She took me to the office. I even got her to close the door while I called. This year was going to be a piece of cake. Mom picked up, and I told her I was going to Evan's and that his dad would drop me off by dinnertime.

On the school bus to Evan's, I told him all about *The Bard's Tale II*. He listened carefully.

"I don't give a shit about that game," he said.

"Yeah," I said. "But there's a troll that does like 490 points of damage."

His red eyebrows rose. "Four hundred ninety points of damage?"

He looked out the window for a minute. Then he looked back at me. "The troll did 490 points of damage? In a single blow? Are you sure?"

I nodded.

"That would . . ." He paused, closed his eyes. His lips moved rapidly without sound, as if he were calculating something in his head.

"A blow like that would push a character all the way down to nothing," he whispered. "And it would keep going."

I nodded rapidly, though I didn't understand.

"Four hundred ninety points of damage would push a character down below human level," he said.

This was real *D&D* calculation I was hearing. I nodded.

"Down below the level of orcs, down below the level of wolves. I don't know."

He blinked at me.

"Down to demon level maybe."

"I've thought about it a little," I said cautiously.

The bus stopped at a light. It was too hot. Outside the windows, giant trees put what they were into the dead air. Inside, the heat vents raised the temperature of the plastic seats. They heated the hard bus plastic until it began to smell.

Evan looked at me expectantly. The bus started moving.

"I've thought about some things 490 points of damage could be like," I said slowly. "If someone, say with an ax, were to hit you for 490 points, your head would like—"

Evan scoffed. "What are you *talking about*?"

I felt confused.

"Yeah, I mean we're talking about what we think 490 points of damage would be like, I just—"

"You can't know by *thinking* about it," he said. "Don't you know that?"

He stared at me intently. My head nodded rapidly, uncontrollably.

"Don't you know *shit*," he hissed. "Stop nodding, freak!"

I stopped with an effort. I suddenly wanted to get off the bus. Why was I there? And why did I keep nodding? My neck ached. My head sat loose and sore in its socket.

I suddenly wished Eric were there. John. Anyone. Evan laughed in my face.

"You *thought about some things 490 points of damage could be like*, huh?" he snarled. "Like a baby getting hit by a truck, maybe? Yeah? Maybe that's like 200 points? And then the truck reverses back and forth over it? Think that would be like 490 points of damage?"

He looked at me with naked disgust.

"Four hundred ninety points of damage isn't *like* anything, pussy!"

"But you said that stuff about the demon level and—"

He waved his hand dismissively.

"I don't have to wonder and compare like you," he said. "My *mom* doesn't take my games away. When we get to my house I'm going to show you *Ultima III*. The whole game takes place on the demon level."

"Oh," I said.

I'm going to learn a lot from this guy, I told myself.

I sat and held my head still and looked at the wrinkled green plastic back of the seat in front of me. It was getting hotter. The smell of heated plastic bus seats doesn't smell like anything else. It isn't like any other kind of smell. Humans can smell it, but it's tuned to an inhuman frequency.

Natural smells are all connected. A pint of blueberries reminds us a little of apples, which reminds us a little of apple pie, which smells a little like tea, which smells a little like hay, and a lot of hot hay smells a little like horse manure, and distant horse manure can sometimes smell like new carpets or like marijuana smoke.

But the smell of heated plastic bus seats reminds us of nothing. Our noses wrinkle when we smell it and that's it.

Except now we've smelled it. Now we know it. We will always have it. We will go to our graves clutching it somewhere deep in our brains like a single puzzle piece, like a key, like a hook.

•

"The demon's name is Exodus," said Evan, opening the door to his house.

His computer was set up right in the hallway, on a cluttered desk ten feet from the front door. I stared around, astonished. Piles of shoes littered the floor. Stacks of papers swayed precariously on every elevated surface. Paper grocery bags stuffed with empty soda cans blocked the foot of a wooden staircase that ascended, twisting and carpetless, into gloom.

An enormously obese man sat before the computer. A few wisps of red hair rose from his skull like a pencil sketch of fire. Numbers scrolled down the screen.

"This is Mike, Dad," said Evan.

"Oh, hello!" The man swiveled slowly around in his chair, smiling kindly, blinking.

"We're going to play *Ultima*," Evan said.

"Right-o!"

The man shuffled painfully to his feet, revealing a hunchback. This was a condition I'd read about in fairy tales, but never seen. Not even in a movie. I tried not to stare. Once he was up, the man made for the stairs in jerky, lopsided baby steps that jiggled and spanked the vast bulk below the serenely still head.

I watched apprehensively, wondering what he would do when he got to the tall bags of soda cans lying across the entrance to the staircase in a crazy fence. But the apparently random jerking with which his left foot swung several times higher than his right was in fact an adaptation to his environment. The jerk carried him easily over the tops of the cans, and he stomped up, dragging his right half behind him.

"His job is computers," Evan explained, sitting down before the screen. His fingers flew over the keyboard and the double columns of numbers disappeared.

"There's no other chair," he said, without taking his eyes from the screen.

I stood behind him, fascinated as the title screen flashed up. ULTIMA III: EXODUS

"Here we go," said Evan.

Unlike *The Bard's Tale II*, this game didn't present its world from a character's-eye view. Rather, a flat map covered the screen. Evan's character was represented by a small blinking humanoid figure at the center. As he moved, the map scrolled with him.

"That's a town," he said, pointing to a tiny white house. "That's the sea," pointing to a blue expanse. "That's the mountains. That's a demon. That's the entrance to a dungeon. That's a field of horses. That's a castle. That's a spellcaster. Those are gems."

The map was a thing of unthinkable complexity. As Evan spoke, my eyes adjusted to what at first seemed like a shimmering green-blue field. Now I saw a world, a world striated, spangled, speckled, and grooved with a thousand traces of life.

I had seen flat maps before, of course. But until that afternoon at Evan's house, I'd never seen what a flat map could do. I'd never been made to understand a flat map's great advantage over reality. In the 3-D landscapes of reality, human vision is shackled to the stumbling motion of the human body. The eye stabs futilely at horizons. Over a journey of minutes and hours you watch hills and houses slowly grow larger before you, and then slowly grow smaller behind. In 3-D, you live under the bitter dominion of distance.

Walking around in 3-D, most of the lines and colors and shapes you see are tricks of perspective. A house looks one way from the front, another from atop a nearby hill, still another from the side. In 3-D, in order to properly recognize something, you have to disregard much of what you actually see.

"I didn't realize that was you! Your head looks so big in this light."

"That's the house? I don't remember it having so many windows."

In 3-D, looking too carefully can be a problem. In 2-D you can never look carefully enough. On a flat map everything appears as it is. Every line and shape on a flat map is charged with significance; a dot conceals multitudes. When you study a flat map, your human vision reaches its true potential and meaning floods the visible.

It's true you have to give up some things. The Grand Canyon is not as impressive on a map as in 3-D. The most detailed flat map cannot give you the visceral thrill of your own smallness that even a moderately sized mountain can.

But a flat map lets you see the world as a *world*. Cultures and conflicts twist across a flat map. A flat map even shows time, condensing centuries of history into borders and capitals, millennia of geology into mountain ranges and sea ridges. To let your eyes wander over a flat map is to travel in time and space, to travel without boredom, without fatigue. More than travel. Just to see the tense squiggle drawn between countries is to feel the blood thrill of conquest and resistance. To see the dot of a city by a lake is to imagine towers.

A flat map by itself is practically already a game. The people who invented chess and *Risk* and *Monopoly* realized this. A flat map is fun in its purest state.

"What's in that town?" I asked, pointing at the far edge of the screen.

"Hints," said Evan. "I've already been there."

"Hints?"

"Clues." He sounded irritated. "The townspeople gave me clues. I'm looking for the demon."

"But we just killed a demon."

"No," Evan said. "I killed *a* demon. I'm looking for *the* demon. Exodus."

"Oh."

I watched him maneuver his avatar over the map. It was amazing.

"Can I play now?"

Evan turned around from the screen. He looked at me.

"Michael."

"Yes?"

"This isn't really a game for two players."

Then he smiled.

That was pretty much the last time Evan ever spoke to me. He stopped telling me the names and the meanings of the marks, lines, and dots that covered the map. He stopped narrating the goals that drove him relentlessly over the landscape in search of the demon Exodus. It was as if he had forgotten I was there.

I didn't care. I watched the screen with eyes the size of worlds.

Minutes and hours passed. Evan's character moved across

the map, which was swiss-cheesed with dungeons and castles and cities, openings through which he'd pass into brown and red spirals concealing monsters, exiting back out onto the blue-green freedom of the map.

The room grew dark except for the fitful light of the monitor. It was silent except for the creak of Evan leaning forward in his chair, the soft whir of the computer's fan, and a ragged wheezing. In the middle of a fierce battle with orcs, I suddenly thought, *Am I wheezing?*

Then it happened again. It wasn't me. It wasn't Evan. It wasn't the computer.

It was Evan's father. He was standing right beside me. I didn't know how long he'd been there. His bulk loomed in my peripheral vision. A half cough imploded softly within him.

He was very close. I couldn't tell what he was doing.

I had never had a foreign adult stand so close to me in silence.

I risked a quick glance and saw Evan's father's eyes fixed intently on the screen. Lit up in his red-rimmed skull, pupils moving. He was watching Evan's character (called "Evan") as he pursued his demon.

I shifted my eyes back to the monitor but I couldn't focus. I couldn't stop thinking that at any moment Evan's father might turn to look at me in silence and would *look at me* while I stood there, silent, unable to break the silence, and he said nothing. Wheezing. Looking.

The only way to stop this from happening was to keep my eyes firmly on the computer screen.

Evan's father and I watched *Ultima III* Evan together.

When *Ultima III* Evan's hit points dwindled down to nearly nothing during a particularly tough battle, we watched.

When *Ultima III* Evan discovered a new town, we watched.

When *Ultima III* Evan gleaned a particularly crucial hint during a conversation with a blacksmith in the town, we watched.

Our breathing synchronized.

I forgot who I was.

•

Then at last Evan's father's arm shot out and hit a switch, and the lights flooded on, and I was back in a 3-D world safely in my own place with an adult who was speaking, filling the air between us with a comfortable fence of words.

"Well, all right, Evan—now, that game sure looks fun, but Mike (it's Mike, isn't it?)—must be time for Mike to get on home to get his dinner, matter of fact it's time for ours, be happy to drive you, Mike, just give me a sec here to put my boots on."

I drank up his words in relief. The uncanny *melded* feeling I'd had standing there lost in the silence watching together with him vanished. No one ever forgets who he is in a conversation. "That's you over there" is what we really say when we speak to each other. "And this is me right here." That's why conversations are so relaxing. That's why people talk so much.

"Oh, thanks," I said loudly. "I guess it is time for me to be getting home. My mom will have dinner ready."

"Well, yes, it probably is that time," Evan's father said. "Getting late now, been dark for a while now, probably should be going."

Evan turned from the screen and smiled at us.

"I'll just stay here," he said.

Evan's father looked at him, confused. "You're not coming?"

"No."

His father looked at him, looked at me, smiled uneasily. "Guess it'll just be the two of us!"

I looked at Evan.

"We could talk about *Ultima III* in the car," I said desperately.

He turned back to the screen.

"Well, hey," I said with bitterness, "thanks a lot for everything. I'll see you in school!"

Evan's father's car was a long gray station wagon stuffed with papers. Boxes of papers crammed the backseats. I had to sit up in the front with him. I even had to help him get his seat belt on. I had to press the belt into his gelatinous flank and ram the head into the buckle while he giggled.

"Oooh, I'm getting big! Thanks, Mike. Safety first! If Evan were here, he'd do it."

We drove off.

"Guess Evan's busy," he muttered.

I gave him directions and he swayed the massive car around the three dimensions of reality. The heat was up way too high.

"What do you think of that game?" Evan's father asked softly. "What do you think of the demon Evan's chasing?"

I looked at him out of the corner of my eye. He was sweating a little in the heat. His face looked sweaty.

"Uh, I don't know, sir."

"You don't have to call me sir," he said. "Just call me Evan. Call me Mr. Evan."

He chuckled. I gripped the side of the seat so tightly I thought my knuckles would burst out of my skin.

"Tell Mr. Evan what you think of that game," he whispered.

"You can let me out here!" I called out.

He braked the car to a halt, squinted down the block. "Which one is it?"

I pointed randomly out the window. "This one!" I undid my seat belt.

Mr. Evan peered at the stucco house with no lights on.

"Is anyone home?" he asked dubiously. "Do you want I should wait till your folks get home?"

"Oh, they're home," I said opening the door. "They're just sleeping. Napping."

I jumped out into the wonderful cold night air, stood on the curb waving frantically at Mr. Evan's car until he drove off. Once his taillights had vanished around the corner, I took three deep breaths. I let out a big, crazy smile of freedom.

Those people are fucked-up, I thought.

I was only eight or nine blocks away from home. It was six-thirty. I had an hour till dinner.

The snowy lawns of the block were lit by streetlamps. The snow emitted a bluish radiance not unlike the screen of a computer monitor. Observing the snow-covered lawn beneath me carefully, I saw it was spangled with marks. Paw prints, boot prints, twig pieces, chunks of black slush kicked up from the road, fallen icicles.

Looking closer, I discovered that even the smooth, unbroken patches of snow between the twigs and footprints were anything but smooth. The snow was gently *waved* in places. In other places you could see the bump from a knob in the underlying earth. A spear of dead grass poked through here. A needle fallen from an evergreen lay there. And there were little mini-drifts of blown powder distributed over the flat spots.

The map scrolled beneath me. Chunks of road salt along the curb were villages, sprung up along a river. And here, in the center of an indentation left by a big adult boot, was a vast canyon. The canyon floor was patrolled by wolves. An oddly shaped chip of asphalt rose from the center of the footprint. A tripartite ebony tower. It commanded tribute from the river towns. And here was the narrow winter road where a long line of donkeys carried the gold of the towns down into the canyon. A demon lived in the tower.

On the far side of the canyon, five crystal cities (five fallen icicles) rise from the plain. One of them is called The Heart of the Light. The center of the city glows. It glows through its translucent length. The city is like a frozen upright river. The people are like frozen waves. They are not human. They are turns and ebbs and waves in light like water. A population liquefied, a people in liquid state. Their city is The Heart of the Light.

They make a solid champion by throwing waves around a bone. Like you throw horseshoes around a stake. Their champion looks a little like the Michelin Man. He will defend the city's honor. He waddles out to the plain between The Heart of the Light and the next city of crystal, which has a name I can't pronounce. The liquid population watches their champion through the open windows; the whole city is an open window. I flexed my cold hands in my mittens.

The river towns, the canyons, the plain of crystal cities all lay on a three-foot-wide square of lawn directly below my nose. The sidewalk, a vast ribbon of desert winding through the center of the universe, lay eight feet to the north. The river of the curb lay just to the south. Between the canyon and the sidewalk desert I could see mountain ranges, fertile farmlands, enormous castles.

I could see millions of lives without moving my neck. I could see centuries of history.

Slowly, I looked up.

I raised my eyes ten millimeters.

I felt faint.

A whole new continent lay on the other side of the sidewalk. An incredible complex structure—it must have been fashioned by demons—loomed out of it. The structure was itself covered with countries—the wood of the porch, the tile of the porch roof—and contained dozens of continents within. I saw eighteen cities in its shadow. Valleys too numerous to count.

I turned my neck, uncovered more continents. I lifted my head and looked down the block. Jesus!

The 2-D world I could now see before me could easily swallow a hundred earths.

It was too much. I dropped my eyes back to my feet, began gently unscrolling the map, mere inches at a time, passing my eyes over villages, ruins, ancient feuds, caravan routes, battlegrounds, lost islands, cathedrals, the skeletal remains of giant wings, houses . . .

•

The police picked me up six blocks from home.

"You Michael Clune?"

I looked up at the cop car, startled. The window was rolled down and the cop peered out. He reached back and popped the rear door open.

"Climb in, your ma's worried sick."

I got in and he turned the cruiser around, rolled it slowly down the street to the lit porch where my mother and sister stood waiting.

"Where you been?" the cop asked, looking back at me in the rearview mirror. "Dawdling?"

It was hard to meet his eyes. I was still adjusting to 3-D.

"Yes," I said. "I was just walking home from my friend's house. I'm sorry."

The cop got out and opened the door for me as my mother came rushing down.

"*Where have you been?*" she shrieked. "It's almost nine o'clock at night."

"Dawdling," the cop said.

"Thank you so much, Officer," said Mom.

"Why'd you call the cops?" I asked as we went up the path.

"Your father is out at a *business function*," Mom said angrily. "You think I'm going to leave your sister alone in the house and go out in the dark searching the streets for you? What in God's name have you been doing?"

"I was just . . . wandering," I said.

In the Garden of Eden, before the fruit of the tree of knowledge had shown them who they were, Adam and Eve *wandered.*

"Wandering?" Mom yelled. "*Wandering?* With your sister and me sitting here worried sick that you'd been abducted? That for all we knew you were dead in some pervert's trunk? Evan's father said he dropped you off *two hours ago.*"

We were in the front hall of our 3-D house now, bright yellow light falling on the angles of my mother's rage.

"You called Mr. Evan?" I said in dismay.

"His name's Robert. And you still haven't answered me. What in God's name were you doing for the past two hours out there in the dark?"

It was a pretty good question. What had I been doing?

But a better question was: *Who had I been?*

I'd been wandering the imaginary maps of the suburban lawns for hours, but what was I? Who had tracked the progress of armies over plains? Who had counted the demons he faced in dark towers? Who had seen the wings of dragons? Who had rescued villagers from the dominion of evil lords?

As I'd passed over different parts of the map, I'd explored the lands through different beings. Historians. Adventurers. Generals. Princesses. Demons. Were these entities imaginary parts of me? Were they character types I'd read about and projected into my fantasy maps?

It didn't matter. The point is that I'd been doing all kinds of things—fighting, exploring, hiding, looting, rescuing, speaking—I'd been *doing* all this without there being a single *doer* to bind all these actions together.

A map splays out such a vast range of possible experiences that it overloads the capacities of any individual. Looked at with a game-ready eye, the map consists of thousands of interlocking adventures. Evan's game trained my eye for maps. Now, as my vision passes over and participates in a map's multiple forms of life, I become two people, ten people, a hundred.

The map-based computer role-playing game is a spiritual device for separating action from ego. Freeing movement from the narrow prison of character.

The Garden of Eden is a flat map.

While I was wandering the Edenic maps of Evanston, Evan remained hunched over his keyboard, shackled to a pixilated version of himself. Exiled from Eden. The map drew explorers, kings, adventurers, knights, and wizards through the thin membrane of my weak personality. I multiplied and became legion, freed for new forms of life and movement. But Evan saw the imaginary map only through the thick bars of his character.

Evan had character. Evan had character that went all the way through him like the color of coal goes all the way through a piece of coal. He didn't need conversation to remind him of the difference between himself and someone else. He was as solid as a bar of metal. Pure Evan. If you cut him, red fluid Evan would leak out. If you dropped an atom bomb on him, tiny Evans would rise in a red vapor from the crater.

Humans with character like that are rare. People think they like that kind of character in a person. "Harry Truman had character." "Ronald Reagan had real character." But they don't. Not really. Successful presidents have the weak character of the protagonist of a light romance. Luke Skywalker. Frodo. Easy to identify with, no hard edges, as capacious a prison as possible.

But in *Star Wars*, Darth Vader is the fascinating one. In Milton's *Paradise Lost*, Satan is the one who fascinates. The one with character. Evan had character like that. He had it so deeply he couldn't escape himself even in fantasy. He didn't have the desire to be someone else. He didn't play games to escape himself. He played games to take himself to new places. To spread. He even gave his avatar his own name, for God's sake. Out of a hundred computer-game players, only two or three will play like that. Only two or three can.

Evan's character made people fear him. It made people hate him. Even me.

•

The school's rebellion against Evan's unassimilable character reached a crisis one day after basketball practice. I was there in spite of myself. I didn't particularly like basketball, I wasn't particularly good at it. My parents thought it was healthy for me. But I'd been able to avoid playing in public school because you actually had to try out for the team, a process that easily weeded me out. But once I was back among the Catholics and their degraded we-take-anyone attitude, there was no avoiding the team.

Eric and John were the stars. Eric was the tall center, John the fast guard. When you looked at Eric or John as they were running across the court, what instantly struck you was that they *wanted* to be running. It was written all over their faces. They *couldn't wait* to get to the other end of the court. They just had to get their hands on that ball.

In short, Eric and John had what the coach called "Hustle." Hustle is not something that can be taught. As soon as it was time for me to start running, for example, all I could think about was when it would be time to stop running. John and Eric loved the ball, they'd run a hundred miles to get their hands on it. I hated the ball. Hate is too strong a word. I felt an aversion to the basketball. I saw it as a kind of round red coach forever screaming, "Run here! Run here! Get over here, Clune! Hustle! Run faster!"

I fantasized that the ball would run out of air, that it would land with a saggy plop on the court and stay put. I fantasized about taking a shot and missing the basket by so much that the ball simply disappeared.

"Clune with the rebound, he steps back, turns . . . no one's open, folks! The shot clock's running down, he turns, fakes, and shoots! This one's waaaaaay over the basket, folks! Jesus Christ, I think it's gone! I think the ball's gone! The refs can't find it! They're waving their hands! Game over! Game over!"

I didn't have Hustle. But I wasn't the worst player on the team, and I was friends with everyone, so they didn't get on my case too bad when my lack of Hustle cost us out on the court.

I did my best, I'd think, jogging to the bench when Coach pulled me out for missing an easy play.

John was standing by the bench, angry, yelling. "Christ, Clune, what the fuck was that?"

I looked at him with steady eyes. "I did my best, John."

"Yeah," said Eric, panting. "Mike did his best."

"But he didn't even *try*," John whined.

"I tried to try," I told him sternly. "Not everyone has the ability to try. It's a gift. And if you have it, then you should be grateful and shut your fucking mouth."

"Yeah," said Eric.

Evan had Hustle. Like everything else about him, his presence on the team was a mystery. But he was as free to join as anyone else, and once on the court, he actually performed pretty well. He wasn't a star like John or Eric, but he wasn't bad. And he was getting better. Every game, he'd hit a few more baskets, grab a couple more rebounds.

It drove John crazy. John wasn't a bad guy, but he had a bit of a chip on his shoulder. And he was especially sensitive to whatever it was about Evan that made even mellow, pleasant kids grind their teeth.

One day at practice, after an unusually stellar performance from Evan, the coach announced his intention to start him the next game.

Evan turned to John and smiled.

"You can't start him, Coach!" John shouted.

The coach flicked an irritated glance at John. "I'll do whatever the hell I want, who do you think you are? And why don't you stop picking on Evan? Give me ten laps."

The rest of us filed out of the gym and everyone hit the showers. Except for me. I was cool and sweatless after another Hustle-deficient practice. I sat on the bench calling out jokes to the guys in the showers when John came in, his handsome freckled face suffused with anger.

"Where's the faggot?" he called out.

"I think Coach is still in the gym," I said.

"I'm not in the mood for your bullshit, Clune," John said with gritted teeth. He strode over to the showers and yanked back the curtain.

"Get out here, faggot!"

He stood with clenched fists, pulsing.

One by one the guys filed out grabbing towels and smirking. At last came Evan. His smile cut through the steam. He stood at the shower entrance with a towel around his waist, arms crossed, smiling.

"You're a *faggot*," John spat at him.

"Oh, leave him alone," said Eric.

"You're just pissed he did better than you in practice," I said.

"I heard your mom is sick, John," said Evan softly.

Everyone shut up fast. John looked like he'd been shot.

"*What did you say?*" he managed finally.

"I said, I heard your mother is pretty sick," said Evan.

His smile got wider.

We couldn't believe what we were hearing. John's mother was in the hospital with cancer. The principal included her name in the list of people to pray for every morning.

"What the fuck did you say about my mother?"

A chorus of other voices rang out behind him.

"That's not cool."

"Hey, that's fucked-up."

"What a little freak."

"Evan, you're such a freak."

"Freak."

Evan's smiled waxed by inches.

"You're a bully, John," he said. "I wonder if having a son who is such a bully is good for someone who has cancer? I wonder if a son like you is good for cancer."

He turned his smile slowly around the locker room.

"I think it's probably bad. I think it's probably *real bad*. I sure hope your mom doesn't die, John."

John hurled himself at Evan, pushing him down to the tiled floor of the shower, savagely pummeling his face, neck, and chest. The other kids and I stood around in a half circle, cheering. Evan kicked and clawed.

"He bit me!" John screamed.

He stood up, holding his arm aloft, pointing to the red streak on the bicep. Evan writhed in blood in the corner.

"Fucking pussy *bit* me!" John yelled. "Where's the pussy's clothes?"

"No!" Evan said.

John laughed hysterically. I was laughing too. Eric tossed Evan's cheap bag to John. John walked over to the toilets followed by a shrieking, laughing crew of kids. He dumped the clothes into the toilet.

"Who's gotta take a piss?" he yelled. "Who's gotta go?"

And Chip, Peter, even Eric lined up to send a stream of urine down on Evan's Catholic school uniform.

"Please don't!" Evan yelled, crying now from the shower floor. "My dad can't afford another uniform!"

Everyone laughed.

"Pussy!"

He buried his head in his arms.

At this moment, Dom pushed forward. He tugged on John's shirt. Dom was an obese, slow-moving Italian kid who almost never spoke. No one knew why he was on the team. He never left the bench. During practice he helped Coach gather up the balls. In public school he would have been in special ed.

Now Dom stood there, tugging on John's shirt, his massive face slowly opening.

"I gotta take a dump," he said.

After a long second of shock, everyone began laughing. I had to hold my stomach, I was laughing so hard.

"Dom's gotta take a dump!"

"He's gotta go!"

"Right here, Dom! Come on now!"

And John led him into the stall where Evan's clothes sat stewing in the toilet. And John raised his hands, hushing the kids who looked at each other with laughter-strangled red faces, laughter-drowned eyes, biting down on their lips hard not to laugh, shaking fingers on lips, ssshhh!, squinting, listen, ssshhh, here it comes!

And then the sound. And then the smell hit us and the laughter rushed out of us like God.

"Oh no!"

"Holy shit!"

"Oh my God!"

"Did you see that?"

"Do you smell that?"

"I'm going to fucking die!"

Kids rolled on the floor gasping and screaming and crying with laughter. Lips spit-bubbled with laughter. Chest-heaving silent laughter. Intestine-straightening laughter.

Finally, through the heaves of laughter, I noticed a different sound. My laugh slowed. I looked around. Other kids had noticed too, and were staring around at each other, still smiling under confused eyes.

"What is that?" Chip gasped.

John, now unsmiling, cocked his head, turned toward the shower. Listened.

"It's *him*!"

We all turned to look. Evan was sitting against the shower wall. He was *hissing*. He was hissing like a snake. And now, as everyone went dead silent, the horrible *hissing* echoed through the tile shower. Hissssss. Hissssss. Hisssssssssss. Evan hissed through his giant fake smile. It wasn't a human smile. It was a serpent's set fangs. He *hissed* through them.

"Jesus," Eric whispered.

"Look at this crazy faggot," John said, walking over. "What, Evan, so you're a snake now? Are you supposed to be a dragon now, you *Dungeons & Dragons* faggot? You 'bout to do some magic? You gonna kill us now with your secret powers? You a demon?"

Evan kept hissing, crouching now in the shower with the naked lightbulb casting dead light down in a sheet over his face, over his bared teeth, hissing.

John turned around, pointed. "This pussy thinks he's in *Dungeons & Dragons*!"

A ripple of nervous laughter went through us.

"Look! This pussy's transformed himself! He's used his secret powers! He's turned into some *Dungeons & Dragons* shit!"

"What's he turned into, John?" someone yelled.

John looked at Evan crouched naked, hissing.

"It's . . . it's . . . it's the Devil Dork!"

Laughter burst from every chest.

"Devil Dork! Devil Dork! Devil Dork!"

Evan crouches, hisses louder.

•

In Milton's *Paradise Lost*, God will not forgive Satan. He damns Satan to hell for all eternity. Satan thinks this a terrible injustice, the act of a divine bully. He hisses at God and his angels, plots against them. But at his lowest point, he thinks—maybe I should just bow down to God and beg him for forgiveness. He imagines that a sincere apology, rising out of his endless torments, might change God's mind. Then perhaps God will forgive him, welcome him back to heaven, to the society of the angels.

But then Satan reflects that after a while, he'd probably get tired of kneeling to God. He'd probably get sick of the vapid small talk of the other angels. He'd rebel again. He knows himself, he'd definitely rebel all over again. And then he reflects that God, being omniscient, knows this. And that's why God won't forgive Satan even if Satan sincerely asks for it. So Satan figures there's no reason to even try to change.

Satan's character is set. He's a fallen soul. His character goes all the way through him. Like the color of coal goes all the way through a piece of coal. Unfallen souls, the souls of average humans, have the possibility of changing. They are airy, full of spaces, the texture of muffins. The texture of angel food cake. One day they're one way, the next day they're a little different. Unfallen souls have two sides, the present self, which maybe sins. And the future self, which maybe doesn't. You can't damn someone like that forever, no matter what they do. They're not the same forever. Their future is genuinely different from their past.

Fallen souls, however, have only one side. You can walk all the way around them without ever getting to the end. That's why Satan is the strongest character in *Paradise Lost*. He exists in three dimensions, while God, the archangels, and even Eve are two-dimensional.

If you're reading this, Evan, you probably aren't very happy with the way I picture you here at the end. *I've got many more sides to me than that*, you might say. *I'm a real person, not this cartoon, not this devil dork.*

I know you have a rich three-dimensional character, Evan. You always did. But I've searched my memory to find your 2-D face. My penance to you is to create a space here for your two-dimensional self, where you can cast off the strain of three solid dimensions, slip out of the cell of your human character. Into the Edenic flatness of a computer screen.

In my memory I look down at Evan's flat red hissing face. I flip his face over.

On the back is a map.

4.

World War II Has Never Ended

That summer I discovered Hitler. I found him in the center of a map in a computer game called *Beyond Castle Wolfenstein*. I destroyed him with a bomb. Then I started the game over and blew him up again. That's history for you.

My friend Marc had the game. July 1987. He'd grown up a block away from me. When his parents split up, he and his mom moved to Skokie to be near family. For a while I kind of lost touch with him. But by the time classes ended for the summer, I was sick of my school friends. After the whole business with Evan, I needed a break. So I started hanging out with Marc again. I'd take the bus to Dempster and Marc would meet me, then we'd walk the couple miles to his house.

"Damn, it's hot," he said.

"Yeah," I said.

"My mom says the world's getting hotter," Marc said. "She says every summer'll get a little hotter and every winter'll get a little warmer, until one day it'll be summer all year round."

"Man, I could use a fucking Slurpee," I said.

There was a 7-Eleven on the corner of his block. The neon of intense sugars blazed from the shelves. Expensive machines whirred, processing fructose, sunlight, and genuine Alpine ice into twenty-ounce paper cups. Perfect size to support the energy needs of eighty-pound upright insects like ourselves. 1987. We lacked livers, could consume only liquid sugar.

"Aaahh," said Marc.

"Yessssss," I hissed.

The manager eyed us suspiciously over his history book. "You're dripping on my floor. Take it outside."

He looked down at the pictures in his history book, up at us.

These things aren't human, he thought.

"Hey, check it out," Marc said when we got outside.

He took two stolen Snickers bars out of his shorts pocket.

"Awesome," I said.

It was so hot in the sun that the bars were a gooey mess by the time we got the packages open. We stood there with lumps of caramel in our hot throats and chocolate smears on our faces.

"It's like a hot brown Slurpee," I said.

We laughed.

"You look like you been eating shit," Marc said.

We laughed.

"Wanna steal some more?" he asked.

"Nah," I said. I stuck and unstuck my brown fingers. "I can't eat any more candy. I'll puke."

We stood sweltering on the sidewalk.

"Hey, I know," said Marc. "I got something cool back at the house."

"What."

"New game."

"Cool."

We trooped down the street and into his basement. Actual air-conditioning. We had two window units at home, one for my parents' bedroom and one for the kitchen. At Marc's house all the air was conditioned. Pulled through the frozen white heart of the compressor seven times per hour. Over his mother's ashtrays. Over the seat of the toilet. Through the tight curls of the carpet, the loose curls of her head.

I passed the open door of the bathroom, looked into the mirror at my shit-eating face and sweat-plastered hair like a helmet. I touched my head self-consciously, rubbed my fists across my cheeks to get the chocolate off.

"Stop with the mirror, you're like a girl," Marc said.

"Why do you have your computer in the basement, anyway," I said, turning toward him. "It's freezing down here."

I rubbed my bare arms.

We walked into the large open room where he kept the computer. It was an Apple. Light-years ahead of my Commodore 64. The basement room was an appropriate setting for the futuristic machine, with the gentle whir of the AC the only sound. The only color came from two high windows. The windows processed summer into little orange tiles. They dropped into a small orange pile on the white carpet at the foot of the white wall.

Marc got a chair for me from the other room and we sat vibrating to the sugar frequency. Listening to the clatter of his mom's steps in the house above.

"We're going to play *Carmen Sandiego* for a bit, Mom," Marc yelled.

We both stared at the ceiling.

"Okay."

The faintness of her voice located her precisely. Second floor, bedroom. We'd hear her coming down for almost a full minute.

"That's why the computer is in the basement," said Marc, turning it on. "Check this shit out."

I never learned how he got it. I never saw it in a store. It was incredibly primitive even for that time. Primitive maze, a green stick figure (you), with thin gun projecting, and yellow stick figures (them) with helmet-shaped heads to show they were Nazis.

"It's called *Beyond Castle Wolfenstein*," he said. "Hitler's in it. You kill Hitler in it."

W straight, A left, D right, space bar to fire. WAD [space] WAD [space] WAD [space]. I maneuvered my avatar around the maze. Soon the corpses of Nazis littered the screen in piles of yellow lines. The material for an alphabet. Material for history books. I hit enter and entered the next level.

"Now check this out," Marc said.

He reached over and switched on the Apple's tiny speakers. "Just wait."

Another maze flickered to life, helmeted Nazis swarming at me like *Pac-Man* ghosts. Suddenly staccato sounds rattled out of the speakers.

"*Kommen Sie!*"

"*Kommen Sie!*"

"*Kommen Sie!*"

A yellow Nazi threw himself at my gun.

"*Kommen Sie!*"

"They're talking!" I gasped.

Marc nodded delightedly.

"That's *real German*."

I'd never heard a computer talk. *Castle Wolfenstein* was the first computer game to feature voices. And what voices. Each word carved with an ax from a slab of static.

"*Kommen Sie!*"

"That's what Nazis say?"

"Yeah," Marc said. "That is pure Nazi language. Hitler language."

"*Kommen Sie! Kommen Sie! Kommen Sie!*"

It was unreal. We stared at each other, stared at the screen. The yellow Nazis moved across the flat maze, shouting genuine German words. The words were a thousand times more obscene than "fuck," "shit," "cunt." "Fuck," "shit," "cunt" come from Saxon, the ancient Germanic root of English. The Nazi words contain the taboo Saxon syllables like the ocean contains fish. "Fuck" and "cunt" spin in the depths of *Kommen*. With the handle of "fuck" and "cunt" Marc and I could grasp the edges of *Kommen*. But only for a split second, then it slipped. Into Nazi abyss. Each computer Nazi syllable a matrix of obscenity.

The Nazi words came from inside the flat computer Nazis. There is no inside to a 2-D computer image. The words came from the other side of the flat Nazis. From 1943, 1941, 1945.

"Does your mom know about this?" I asked Marc.

"Hell no," he said. "Listen to this shit."

"*Kommen Sie.*" "*Kommen Sie.*"

WAD [space] WAD [space] WAD [space].

Two hours later we maneuvered our avatar into the room with Hitler. We carried the fatal briefcase with the bomb. The explosion shook out of the speakers like *Kommen* turned inside out. *Nnnnemmmmmmokkk!* Hitler minus Hitler.

"What now?"

"We play it again."

The flat Nazis shouted their words out at us from the depths of 1943. I wondered what we sounded like to them.

Nineteen forty-three. Two Nazis carefully approach the castle wall. A green boy's face shimmers on the stone.

"*Kommen Sie?*" they say carefully. "*Kommen Sie?*"

The flat boy ripples.

"WAD [space]," he says.

•

I've stumbled from a dark, cold room into summer after killing Hitler so many times it's hard to believe there was a first time. Marc and I raced up the stairs, fingers and legs numb from the basement air-conditioning, out into ninety degrees of summer.

At the center of summer the world warps. At ninety degrees the trees houses sidewalks lie flat against the sky. Summer is the flattest season. Season of two dimensions, of shapes stuck on a wall of light.

"My mom says every summer it gets hotter," said Marc.

"Won't matter how hot it gets if there's a World War III," I said. "*My* mom says World War III is coming."

Marc snorted.

"Ain't no World War III coming," he said. "Hitler already came."

We walked aimlessly down the block.

"What's the deal with Hitler?" I asked.

"Whaddya mean, what's the deal with Hitler?" Marc said. "Hey, check it out."

A large black plastic squirt gun, molded to look like an M16, lay on the lawn in front of us. Marc grabbed it.

"Whose is it?" I asked.

"Who cares?" he said.

"Ack-ack-ack," he said, aiming the gun at me.

"Hey, I know!" he yelled, dropping it to his side. "Let's play *Wolfenstein*."

"Again?"

It was a great game, but after two straight hours, I needed a break.

"No, man," said Marc. He wiggled the squirt gun at me. "Let's play it for real. With this."

"You seriously want to play pretend war out here with that fucking squirt gun?"

I was almost twelve, for chrissakes.

Marc shrugged.

"No one's out here," he said.

I looked up and down the block. The heat had swept the street clean of human life. An overturned green metal tricycle radiated on the sidewalk.

"*I'm* out here," I said. "And playing pretend war is kiddie shit. Gimme that goddamn gun."

I grabbed it off him, intending to throw it into the bushes. But once I had it in my hands, I was surprised by its weight. This feels kind of like a real gun, I thought. Marc looked at me, smiling.

"C'mon," he said. "There's nothing else to do."

He was right. When you're almost twelve and you've played all the computer games you can play in a day, what can you do? You're old enough to know about stealing, but too young to know about the things worth stealing. There's basically nothing to do. So either you stay bored or you regress a little.

"It'll be like Capture the Flag," said Marc.

I nodded slowly. Capture the Flag was semi-respectable. We'd played it at the day camp I went to last summer.

"Except it'll be Kill the Hitler," he continued. "You get to be the Hitler. I get the gun." He grabbed it out of my loose, unprepared fingers.

"Hey!" I said.

"I'll close my eyes and count to sixty," Marc said. He closed his eyes. "One."

"Hey," I yelled. "I don't know this neighborhood! I don't know where to hide!"

"Two," he counted. "Three."

I looked desperately up and down the block. Nothing but small suburban houses with tiny exposed lawns.

"Six," counted Marc. "Seven."

I ran, heart pounding. Houses and lawns, exposed to the

sun, as far as the eye could see. Fuck, I thought. Fuck. I stopped, clenching my fists. Chill the fuck out, I told myself. What would Hitler do?

I ran to the end of the block. Turning the corner, I saw concrete steps at the side of a house, leading down into a sunken stairwell. The stairs to somebody's basement. I ran over, jumped the iron railing, landed hard on my shoes on the concrete slab six feet below street level.

The stairwell smelled moldy. There was a dead bird in the corner. But I was out of sight, and I discovered that by crouching down against the wall, I had a clear view of the sidewalk. Not the sidewalk itself, exactly, but the air above it.

A head sailed clearly into view, the white-haired head of an old man, grimacing in the heat. In a few seconds he was gone. I can see them, I thought, but they can't see me. Not unless they actually walked to the edge of the stairs and looked down. If they did that, of course, I'd be defenseless.

Not quite defenseless, I thought. A four-foot length of iron railing had fallen into the stairwell. Now I picked it up, felt its satisfying weight. It was about the same length as a gun, I thought. I experimented with aiming it. But whatever way I turned it, the railing felt best and most satisfying when I gripped it like a baseball bat.

This is for clubbing people over the head with, I thought. Not for shooting with.

The stairwell was out of the sunlight, but it collected heat like an oven. Sweat dripped into my eyes. I imagined Marc sticking his head over the edge of the stairwell. I could use the railing as a pretend gun and aim for the whites of his eyes. Or I could use it as a pretend club and club his head to mush with it.

I realized then that we hadn't agreed on the rules of the game. Did he just have to pretend shoot me, and that was it?

Couldn't I defend myself? If I tagged him before he tagged me, would I win? And what did *tagged* mean in the context of this game? Shooting? Clubbing?

We were playing *Wolfenstein*. I thought about the rules of that game. The player tried to kill Hitler any way possible, and Hitler and his Nazis tried to kill the player. They used guns, knives, even their bare hands. *Kommen Sie!*

Adrenaline shot through me. Sweat ran in rivers down my face. I stared up at the sidewalk. Marc could be playing by real *Wolfenstein* rules and come jumping over this railing down at me any second, I thought. Stomping down at me. I looked fearfully up at the air. And Marc isn't the only one, I thought. My breath caught in my throat. Whose house is this? I thought. I don't know anyone around here, I thought.

I am no longer on public property, I realized with horror.

I remembered my parents arguing about a shooting that had been reported in the newspaper a few months ago. Dad kept saying, *But it wasn't on public property, he was on private property, Barb, the victim had left public property and entered private property when he got shot, that's what happened, Barb.*

I crept up the stairs and crouched, peering at the public sidewalk through sweat and terror. It was at least ten feet away. Ten feet of private grass at least. And then this private railing, and all this private concrete. Anyone who found me in the stairwell would have a perfect right to do anything they liked with me. I dropped back down. I gripped the railing-club tighter.

Heads had been passing this whole time. They looked yellow in the sun. All the people out there in the sun, I thought. Their heads were yellow with it. Rotten with it. Their round, white-haired, black-haired, curly, bald heads rotted to the core by the sun.

Soon the heads starting coming faster. From where I crouched, looking up over the wall of the stairwell, over the railing, all I could see were the heads. Sometimes just the very tops of the heads. Little kids, I assumed, or midgets maybe. Sometimes a tall one would come by, and I could see some of the neck. But mostly I just saw the heads. A procession of heads. Not whole heads, even; all I could see were the profiles bobbing by. Flat profiles, like ugly presidents on hot coins.

I imagined one of the flat heads turning, thinning as it turned. I imagined the head turning completely on its flat side to reveal an ultra-thin knife's edge, aimed at my eyeball. These heads have flat sides and thin edges, I thought giddily. They're like switchblades, I thought. Switch-heads.

Then the sight of a particularly slow-moving head jolted me out of my reverie. *Is that Marc?*

I squinted, rubbed the sweat out of my eye. Crouched further down against the wall, peered up. My eyeballs stung. The head was gone. I couldn't be sure. *There. Now.* Is that Marc? The head paused. It hung there for whole seconds. Trembling with turning-potential. Then it moved on, vanished from my line of sight.

I'd gotten a better look this time. It was about the right height in the air to be Marc's. Curly hair like Marc's. At least I thought it was. Hard to tell, the sun just blurred and yellowed everything all to hell up there. And the head size. Same size head as Marc's? Hard to tell.

How big was Marc's head? Compared to what? I closed my eyes, imagined his head in the basement. Was it bigger or smaller than the computer monitor, for example? I mentally positioned Marc's head in front of the monitor.

It seemed to me then that the monitor was bigger than Marc's head. It seemed to me that the monitor was *much* bigger than Marc's head, that Marc's head would fit comfortably in front of the computer monitor, leaving space around his skull where you could see the other Nazis coming and the maze.

Marc's head could fit *in* or *on* the computer monitor, I thought.

I peered up at the heads floating by on the sidewalk.

And so could any of them, I thought, gripping the length of railing hard. And so could all of them, I thought.

•

In the end I calmed down. After a while I even dropped the railing. Then I calmed all the way down to dead boredom and said *Fuck it* and left the stairwell in disgust. I wandered back, looking for water. Marc was already in the 7-Eleven drinking a Slurpee.

"I guess I won," I said. "Shithead."

"Hitler never wins," said Marc. "I just stopped playing."

"No," I yelled hotly. "Oh no you don't. You couldn't find me! I won!"

"Whatever," Marc said.

I got a bottle of water and a Slurpee. We walked outside and slumped in the shade of the wall.

"Why'd you stop, anyway?" I asked him.

He shrugged.

"*Castle Wolfenstein* in real life," he said, "It just isn't the same as the computer game."

He shook his head.

"I mean, there were all these other people out there. Not doing anything. Not wearing uniforms or anything. And I couldn't ignore them, I had to keep getting out of their way and shit."

He shook his head.

"It sure wasn't like *Wolfenstein*," he said. "It was like watching TV."

When our Slurpees were done, we got up and walked down the block in silence.

"It's like the worst TV show ever," I said finally.

"What," said Marc. "What is?"

"Being out here," I said. "You just said it was like TV. I said, well, if it's TV, it must be the worst TV show ever."

He gave me a funny look.

"That was, like, three hours ago," he said.

"No it wasn't," I said. "You just said it!"

But there were goose bumps on my arm. It was dark out, I realized. It was night.

•

Back home the next day standing next to the kitchen air-conditioning unit, I talked things over with my mom.

"Marc has a computer game about World War II," I said.

"I hope it doesn't have any of that witchcraft in it, like that other game you had," she said darkly. "I hope you're not playing that awful game with those *runes* again, Michael."

"No, Mom. It's called *Castle Wolfenstein*. You kill Hitler in it. It's historical."

"Oh," she said. "Well, if it's historical."

"World War II was a pretty big deal, huh," I said.

"It sure was," she said. "Ask your grandfather. He fought in it. The whole world fought in it. That's why they call it World War II."

I tried to imagine Grandpa throwing a grenade at Hitler. It was hard.

"What really big has happened in history *since* World War II?" I asked.

She looked surprised.

"Lots of things," she said.

"Like what?"

"Well," she said. "President Reagan got elected. That's historical. And there was the oil embargo in the seventies."

"The oil embargo?"

"That's when the Arabs raised the price of gas. There were gas shortages."

I looked at her to see if she was joking.

"There were long lines at the gas station," she said defensively.

"Long lines at the gas station? That's the big thing that's happened in history since World War II?"

She threw up her hands. "What do you think I am, a history book? I'm trying to get dinner ready for you kids and then I gotta get dressed to go out with your dad and you're standing here bothering me!"

I slumped against the wall. "Sorry for asking. Jeez."

She looked at me gently, as if regretting her explosion. Probably she was reflecting that this was a classic *educational opportunity,* the kind only bad mothers let slip.

"Big things *are* still happening in history," she said. "In fact, more historical events are happening today than ever before in history."

"Like what?"

"Well, like the Russians, for one. World War III might be coming!" she exclaimed. "If World War III comes, you sure won't be sitting here bugging me saying *Hey, Mom, why has nothing happened in history since World War II?*"

"*If* World War III comes," I said. "Marc says there's not ever going to be a World War III. He says World War II was it."

"And just how does Marc know that?"

I shrugged. "I told you. He's got a computer game about it."

Mom snorted.

"Well, World War III *is* coming," she said. "Oprah had a history professor on the TV the other day, and *he* said that people never learn from the past, and the way the world is going with the Russians and the nuclear bombs there's probably going to be a World War III and it's going to be a lot worse than World War II, that's for sure."

She glared at me.

"Maybe instead of playing computer games with Marc you should be reading history books."

"Why should I read a stupid old history book?"

Now I was just being difficult. Mom took the bait, turned to me with her hands on her hips.

"People who don't learn about the past are doomed to repeat it," she said.

"But if there's no World War III," I said smugly, "if there's just World War II and no World War III and World War II is all we've got, then we *have* to repeat it."

"You're just being a brat now," Mom said wearily, turning back to the stove.

"And that's why it's *good* for me to play computer games about World War II," I said triumphantly. "We need computer games, *not* history books, because if there's just World War II and that's it, we don't have to worry about not repeating the past. We have to learn how to repeat the past *more* and *better*."

"If you're going to stand in here all day, you can start peeling these potatoes," Mom said.

•

As the years passed, evidence of the truth of *Castle Wolfenstein*'s history lesson accumulated. It turned out that the professor Mom saw on Oprah was wrong and the game was right. By 1993 the USSR was gone and it was clear there would never be a World War III. World War III wasn't coming. World War III had never *been* coming, and the World War III boosters—especially the history professors, with their whole *If you don't learn about the past you can't change the future* shtick—had a lot of explaining to do.

Meanwhile, World War II had never stopped. *Wolfenstein 3-D* came out in the early nineties. I got it during my freshman year in college.

In *Wolfenstein 3-D* you maneuvered down hallways where the walls got smaller in the distance like real hallways. That was the 3-D part. There was a gun sticking out at the bottom of the screen to show you were a person. At the ends of the hallways were flat Nazis with shotguns, grenades, machine guns. And at the end of the game there was a giant 2-D Hitler in a 3-D room. He had Gatling guns for arms.

WAD [space] WAD [space] WAD [space].

I was taking Modern American History. I was interested in history. In class we learned that World War II had put an end to the Great Depression. That World War II had generated most of the major scientific and technical breakthroughs of the century, from atomic energy to the transistor to penicillin. That the wartime partnership of the United States and the USSR against Hitler had prefigured and in fact completely stolen the thunder of the collapse of Communism into capitalism that most people associate with 1989. We began to see that Modern American History is the history of World War II.

Then one day the history professor drew a straight line across the blackboard. At the far left he put a dot with "WW2" above it. Then he proceeded to draw other dots, and above the dots he wrote the names of such pseudo events as "Oil

Embargo," "Watergate," "*Challenger* Explodes," and "Bill Clinton Elected."

"History continues to move forward," he intoned.

But history continued to not move forward. Six years later I was out of college and in grad school. By that time everyone knew the world was getting flatter. *The World Is Flat* was an international bestseller. History had attained the condition of a computer-game screen. But since we didn't yet understand the nature of computer games, most people were as clueless about history as the history professors.

Return to Castle Wolfenstein came out just in time. The seasons were collapsing into summer. The world was getting flatter. Compared with *Wolfenstein 3-D*, the graphics were more detailed, the levels more elaborate. This was a World War II rich and detailed enough to live in.

I put away my books and addressed myself full-time to *Return to Castle Wolfenstein* between August and October 2001. September 11 erupted in the dead center of my playing, but I wasn't distracted. The history professors and television people predictably seized on the tragedy as evidence that big things can still happen in history, that history is still moving forward, that the WAR ON TERROR will finally free us from the orbit of World War II, that the WAR ON TERROR is the real World War III, that we have to learn from the past so we don't repeat it, that we are *now living through real new history, that our species can still make history, that we have now finally entered a real new history-making war.*

I wasn't distracted by the September 11 hype. I was serious. I was studying for a PhD, after all, and I knew that I could learn more about the past, more about the present and the future, by playing *Return to Castle Wolfenstein* for two months straight than I could by reading a hundred history books.

I put my lips to the screen and spoke into the flat world.
WAD [space].

World War II accepted me. For two full months I was a soldier. I saw a hell of a lot more action than Grandpa ever did.

I remember running across a paved courtyard while Nazis shot at me from the windows.

I remember a corridor leading to a vast room. Stained glass windows in the east wall. A picture of Hitler on the west wall. The picture concealed a secret door. It opened, revealing an elevator.

I remember cable cars moving over Alpine expanses.

I remember vaulted ceilings.

I remember machine gun nests at the top of stone stairways.

My phone rang once a day, then once a week. It stopped sometime in September.

There was a picture of Hitler on the west wall. When you pressed the center, his face cracked, opened, fell away. There was an elevator on the other side.

Hitler minus Hitler.

When you take away Hitler from Hitler, there is not nothing. There is an elevator. You press the button in the elevator and it ascends. The ghost of your face is in the screen. When you awake, you exit the elevator. You are in your apartment.

•

But it wasn't until 2004, seventeen years after those summer afternoons with Marc, that I finally grasped the full measure of *Castle Wolfenstein*'s history lesson. In 2004, *Call of Duty* came out, *Wolfenstein*'s greatest successor. I'd been off computer games for two and a half years. My professors and so-called friends had broken me. They'd convinced me that if I didn't give up computer games I'd never finish my dissertation. I'd never be able to afford nice clothes. I'd never be able to go on vacations.

None of that stuff was appealing to me. But they did manage to plant an irrational fear of computer games in my head. A superstitious fear that computer games were sucking my life dry instead of nourishing it. Deadening my brain instead of illuminating it. Burying facts under fiction. Life under fantasy. History under the clatter of computerized gunfire.

The first time I saw it was at Best Buy. I'd gone there to get some printer paper. They'd rearranged the store, so there were cell phones where the paper should have been. I walked to the next aisle. More cell phones. The next aisle: a wall of shining computer-game boxes. Most of the boxes bore the legend *Call of Duty*. The box featured an image of a soldier firing into a swarm of Nazis. I leaned closer, breathing hard.

The front of computer-game boxes never show actual images from the game. They show an artist's conception of the game action. Bold colors, realistic faces, the light of distant explosions reflected on the barrels of guns. The computer-game player looks *through* the cover image. The cover image is a representation of the game. They never show the game on the front of the box. The game isn't made to be looked at. The game is a way of looking. A way of moving. A way of wanting.

I stared through the cover of *Call of Duty* into World War II. The image on the cover of a computer game, like all flat things, has a back side. The back of the box shows actual screen shots. Views of the world from within the game. When you look at the front of the box, you still have your own eyes. The back of the box shows you your new eyes. I reached out my hand . . .

Froze. What was I doing? What would happen to me? I'd

been making good progress on my dissertation. Could my new productive life sustain immersion in World War II? Could I look Hitler in the face again? What would it do to me?

I turned and walked quickly out of the store. I borrowed paper from my girlfriend.

But I didn't forget. I began inventing reasons to go to Best Buy.

"Hey, Kara," I said. "You want to go look at some new dryers?"

"What?" she said.

"Don't you want to get a new dryer?"

"We don't have money to get a new dryer."

"Well," I said, "but we could just look. It's fun to look, isn't it?"

"Fun to look at dryers? Are you high?"

I went by myself to look at the dryers. They had giant round screens in the front. I could imagine Hitler in there. You'd spin him to death.

•

Kara got the flu. I stayed home all weekend, bringing her Theraflu and 7-Up and NyQuil.

"You're out of NyQuil, honey," I said, tossing the empty bottle into the garbage can.

She coughed weakly from the bed. "Oh, could you get me some? This cough, I can't sleep . . ."

I nodded, grabbed my keys, smiling. There was a drugstore across the street from the Best Buy. Not the *nearest* drugstore, maybe. But the best drugstore. I got in my car and drove. I drove straight past the nearest drugstore. Then I drove straight past the best drugstore, straight into the Best Buy parking lot. Walked briskly into the store, jogged past the beautiful dryers, past the aisle where the printer paper used to be. To the *Call of Duty* aisle. This time I didn't hesitate. I answered the Call. When I got home, I realized I'd forgotten the NyQuil. Kara was asleep.

While waiting for the computer to load, I looked through the game manual. "To move forward, press W," it read, "A to turn left, D to turn right. Press [space] to jump." My stomach tightened. I gasped when the game flickered to life. The level of detail was incredible. The Nazis had a gigantic vocabulary and they threw genuine German grenades. The men my grandfather fought with in World War II called the German grenades "potato mashers." They looked like little hammers, he told me. The Nazis in *Call of Duty* threw grenades that looked just like little hammers.

I ran through the corridors and across the fields of World War II, dodging grenades, shooting Nazis. Pursuing objectives. Making history. In the *Castle Wolfenstein* games you'd always operated as a solo agent, infiltrating the enemy stronghold, killing Hitler, escaping. The great innovation of the *Call of Duty* series was the addition of comrades. Now, when you ran across a field or through a secret SS castle, you were accompanied by fellow soldiers. I'm not talking about multiplayer. I'm not talking about actual people from Iowa or New York City playing together on the Internet pretending to be soldiers. I'm talking about real comrades, real soldiers. The computer generated them. They shot with you, ducked with you, died with you.

Of course this *belonging* was always implicit in the World War II game genre. It was the meaning of your soldierhood, after all. But *Call of Duty* made it explicit. Highlighted it. Your fellow soldiers even had names. Yes sir, Sergeant Jones! To me, Private Winarski!

As I played, the electricity in my stomach uncoiled, pushed

through my veins, glittered in my knuckles, tingled on the back of my neck. It wasn't fear anymore. It was excitement. No, it was relaxation. No, excitement. Tanks, mazes, planes, elevators, ammunition depots, burning cities. Yes, Sergent Jones! Watch out, Winarski!

WAD [space] WAD [space] WAD [space]. My nervous system spun up, the sand of my flesh became glass. My body took a clear tone from the game, like a wineglass tapped by a fork. I remember this feeling, I whispered. Private Winarski turned his flat head around. I know this feeling, I thought. Sergeant Jones pointed.

God, I thought, my fingers flying across WAD [space]. I stole quick glances at the keyboard. God, I thought. A hedgerow ahead, jump! Turn right! Fire! Left, ahead, left again, fire! God, I thought. A tank, shit, right! Forward! Fire! God, I thought, glancing down.

WAD [space], *look* at it. My fingers flew up and down. Across. Up and down, across. WAD [space]. Two lines on the keyboard. W to the [space]. The vertical line. A to the D. The horizontal line. God, I thought. WAD [space]. It looks, I thought (dodge the grenade), God, I thought, it looks just like (run after Sergeant Jones, over the roof, now jump), God, I thought, WAD [space] is a *cross*, WAD [space] forms a *slanted cross* on the keyboard!

And every bullet I shot into a Nazi was a nail. Nailing me to the cross of WAD [space]. Every rocket I fired at a Nazi tank was a nail. Every shotgun blast I sent into Hitler was a nail. Nailing me to the cross of WAD [space]. The cross is the universal symbol of transformation. To be nailed to a cross is to suffer magical transformation. Shoot a Nazi! Shoot a Nazi! Shoot a Nazi! Mystical blood flows from my human wrists! Shoot a Nazi! I hang from the cross of WAD [space]!

World War II games have this advantage over Christianity:

It is not your own suffering that weds you to the cross of redemption. It is the suffering of Nazis.

That night, before I went to sleep, I imagined running across a field with a gun chasing fleeing Nazis. Then my mind's eye panned back, and there were a dozen of us, running across the field chasing the Hitlerites. My mind's eye panned back. There were hundreds of us. Panned back. Thousands. I panned back until I was a dot, then I was less than a dot, then there was only color. A black cross of troops moving across Europe, toward the heart of Germany.

•

I woke up coughing.

"Oh dear," Kara said. She stood above me, bright health shining in her face. "I hope I didn't give you my flu, baby!"

I crawled through internal fog to the computer.

"You should really get back in bed," she said. "You're as sick as a dog."

"Soon," I rasped.

Once I got to the computer, my vision cleared up. My computerized eyes clicked on. I slid off my feet into WAD [space] with relief. Full body motion restored. Quick movements. Strength. I could dodge and shoot even faster than before. My aim was better. I wasn't aware of my fingers anymore. The cross of WAD [space] lay somewhere behind my eyes. I dodged, jumped, and shot by thinking. This flu is a viral interface, I thought. Weaken the flesh, open the mind. This flu is great. They should sell it with the game, I thought.

I had a flamethrower now. Nazis melted. There was a farmhouse I had to run through to cut off their retreat. Sergeant Jones urged me forward. I ran forward. We cut off their retreat, but there were more Nazis in an abandoned mine. You can never get to the top or the bottom of World War II, I thought. Even with a flamethrower. But you can get to the heart. To Hitler. Every road leads to the heart, but you can never get to the top or the bottom of World War II, I thought.

Kara was calling. When I pulled WAD [space] out of my skull it made a wet *thwap*. I sat back, absolutely stupefied. Then the coughing picked me up and shook me like a towel.

The flu lasted a week. Some days I was too weak to sit upright for more than ten minutes. The bare minimum corporeal support necessary for participation in history, I couldn't do it. Alone in my bed, I wept, thinking of the war. I wept in total devastation and isolation, shivering under my blankets, a million miles outside of history. Belonging to nothing. Like a rock on the beach belongs to nothing. Like the people who have somehow wandered out of World War II and walk the malls and office buildings of America.

Why do computer games know that history stopped at World War II? How did computer games discover that history starts again only when World War II starts again? Why do computer games know that history has not stopped only where World War II has not stopped? Why do computer games know more about history than history professors? What are they attuned to that history professors are not?

It's not like *Wolfenstein* was a realistic re-creation of some historical World War II battle or something. No, the truth of the game was more elusive. Computer games about World War II aren't fun because they're true. If you start with what you think is true and then try to make it fun, you'll never get anywhere. That's the *Where in the World Is Carmen Sandiego?* mistake. Computer games about World War II are true because they're fun. True because of how they're fun. The truth inside computer games is the secret inside fun.

Computer games are tuned to the frequency of fun. They

didn't set out looking for the truth of history. They set out for total fun and discovered the truth about history along the way. What's fun? A struggle where you risk everything, sure. Victory in a life-and-death struggle, that's fun. And the struggle has to be immediate, direct. Nothing abstract. We're not talking about acing the SATs here. Or outsmarting a client. We're talking about a man coming at you with a pistol trying to kill you and you have a pistol and a body that can go forward, left, right, or jump. That's fun.

But it's not total fun. Total fun is when you not only kill the enemy, you simultaneously explode into unity with a vast army of grateful others. Total fun is when you are one of the many, and the victory you are fighting for is the truth and feeling and joy and meaning of being one of the many. Total fun is when the enemy tries to subtract your one from the many and you have a pistol or a flamethrower and you subtract him instead, and the thrill is the thrill of the largeness of the many, locked in combat with Nazis.

That's total fun. To be part of a visceral struggle between titanic forces. The abrasion of army against army is the movement of history. To be part of that abrasion. To be a tooth, a groove, an edge on the cutting surface of history. That's totally fun.

Just shooting at people who are shooting at you is fun in itself, of course. Look at *Doom* or *Max Payne* or *Duke Nukem*. Those games are pretty fun. But to shoot at people who are shooting at you as part of a titanic struggle where every bullet you fire simultaneously lifts you up, gathers you into grateful millions all facing the same way against the Nazi wind, that's totally fun. *Castle Wolfenstein, Return to Castle Wolfenstein, Wolfenstein 3-D, Call of Duty, Medal of Honor*. The desire computer games about World War II relentlessly satisfy is the

desire for history. The fun computer games pursue with re-
lentless precision is the human feeling for history.

The computer games know about history because they know
about fun. And the only reason to have history anymore is for
fun. The world doesn't need it. The world has capitalism now, it
doesn't need history. Titanic struggles between vast forces used
to move things around in the world. The Mongol invasion. The
Crusades. The Napoleonic Wars. The Thirty Years' War. These
titanic struggles were the rivers through which goods, ideas,
technology, and art flowed from one land to another.

Now we have the global market. There's no one for us all
to be against, there's no reason for us to think of ourselves as
part of an invincible whole moving irresistibly forward against
our enemies. History doesn't make sense. The objective necessity for history is over. History has stopped. And we can
find out exactly when it stopped. Because when the fun ex-
perts want to make a game that is totally fun, they discover
that the closest time period they can set it in is World War II.

•

Okay, okay, but still. What's the deal with Hitler? How many
times do I have to kill him? I think there's something I still
don't understand about World War II games.

A few days after I got over the flu, Kara left me. She even
took the bed. Her parents and friends came over with a moving truck and took all her stuff, which was basically all the
stuff in the apartment. My books lay piled on the carpet. My
computer sat on the boards of the floor. I didn't know what to
do. I went to Best Buy looking for an air mattress. They told
me to go to Target.

Night comes early in an apartment without lights, without

bookshelves, without tables or a bed. I read a little by the light of the computer monitor. *Pride and Prejudice*, I think it was. Then I turned on *Call of Duty*. It was 1945. We were closing in on Berlin. Hitler was in his bunker. Before the last great battle, the general briefed us.

"Okay, boys, this is it! This is what we've been fighting for these long, hard years. This is what our comrades have died for. This is what it's all come down to. The devil's lair!"

The screen cuts to a picture of Hitler.

"We're closing in on him, boys. He's in a bunker somewhere in the center of Berlin."

The screen shows a schematic of a bunker.

"That's our objective," the general says. "Hitler's down there in that bunker. He's down there deep under the city with his last remaining minions. He's still directing his forces on the surface, he's still communicating with the surface, we're not sure how. But it doesn't matter. We're going to kill him." He lights his cigar. "Any questions?"

At 04:30 hours we pile out of the truck, gripping rifles, grinning.

Meanwhile, in a bunker deep underground, the sole controller of a crumbling empire awakens. His hands are trembling too badly to grip. His eyes are so encrusted with cataracts he can barely see. The sound of calm voices enunciating the details of endless catastrophes stutters and fades in the coils of his ears.

"Report!" he barks to one of his last remaining minions. "Report!"

"Sir?" she says softly.

"Report," he repeats.

"I hear the sound of footsteps to the northwest," she says.

"Whiz," says the leader in the bunker, "Whiz, report."

"I am in the data library, sir," he says.

"Iris," the leader begs, "Iris, what do you see?"

"The walls," Iris says. "The walls of the corridor are sky blue."

"The footsteps are getting louder," warns Auda.

The familiar words scroll down the screen: "You hear footsteps in the room outside your chamber. You see shadowy shapes bent over the controls of your cryogenic suspension tank. Your life support systems have been disabled. You have failed."

"Damn," I curse softly.

They killed me again, I think. How many times has it been? Is there a limit to how many times a person can die? Will I ever stop dying?

The computer screen is dark. The cursor blinks, like a door opening and shutting.

5.

The Sun and the Stars

Throughout my early adventures with computer games, my physical self remained safely and firmly rooted in our old family home in Evanston. In February of 1988 we moved. There were three of us kids now. Me, Jenny, and our newish brother, Sean, who was four. Evanston is a near suburb of Chicago but also a small city in its own right. We moved to the far northern suburb of Mettawa, a quite different kind of suburb. A curiosity of the late twentieth century, Mettawa is a human settlement without a center. No town hall, no library, nothing. A tiny village of large houses and horse farms.

My father's career had gone well enough to indulge my mother's primordial fantasy of horses. So we moved into the smallest house in a district of mansions. Five acres, with stables at the back that sheltered a lazy old trail horse named Charlie Brown and a small pony named Red, who was delivered in the back of a minivan. A few months after depositing us in this refuge, my father divorced my mother and left. One day in June he was standing in the sun, smiling uncertainly at Charlie Brown, and the next day he was gone. That summer morning, Jenny, Sean, and I awoke to find ourselves trapped inside Mom's darkening horse-farm fantasy, with three months until school, no friends, and nothing to do.

It had taken a lot of money to turn Mom's fantasy real. The horses swayed on the grass, swollen with money. When we looked out the bay windows of the breakfast room, the trees stood straight, propped up by scaffolds of money. There was no money left for computer games. At our silent lunches I stared out the window at Charlie Brown grazing in the far field. I reflected that with the money stored in just one of his eyes, I could buy ten or twelve computer games. And I knew just where to buy them. The enormous Hawthorn Mall was a twenty-minute drive from our house, and when Mom had to go to Sears or Marshall Field's, I'd climb in the back of the Suburban. I had no money. I just wanted to be near computer games for a while.

In the Suburban, Bette Midler sang out of the speakers. The Bee Gees sang out of the speakers. The Beatles sang out of the speakers. I lay in the very back, looking out the rear window, the long vehicle behind me like a giant finger stirring trees, pavement, street signs, and cars into the endless blue sky. I lay between the wheel wells and looked out at the sky-tree-pavement-car mix streaming out the rear window until Mom shut off the engine, cutting Bette Midler's voice in half.

"All right kids, everyone out!"

Four doors opened in the cavernous truck and we fell out, dazzled by the sun. The one thing my mother's fantasy did not lack was space. We each had our own door in the car. We each had our own bedroom in the house. We each had our own bathroom, even. In fact, the whole district was full of space. Space-rich. You had to drive forever to get anywhere. There was room for several Evanstons between any two points of interest. And most of the time there was room for an Evanston inside the point of interest itself. Hawthorn Mall, for instance.

"Sean, you stay with me," Mom said. "Jenny and Michael, I want you both back at this entrance in half an hour. Okay? Half an hour. It's two-thirty now. That means I want you back here at three. Okay? Three o'clock."

Jenny and I stood sweltering on the blacktop, blinking at the white mountains of the mall.

"Not four o'clock," Mom continued. "Not three-thirty. I want you back here at three o'clock. That's in half an hour. Thirty minutes. Jenny? What number will the little hand on your watch point to when it's three o'clock?"

"You mean on my Swatch?" said Jenny. She was ten.

"If you sass me again, you can just come to Sears with Sean and I to get towels," Mom said, "Is that what you want? No? Then what number will the little hand point to when it's three o'clock, Jenny?"

"Three," said Jenny.

"And the big hand?"

"Twelve," Jenny replied.

Our conversations in Mettawa were part reality, part fantasy.

"And that doesn't mean three-twelve," Mom continued. "If the little hand is on the three and the big hand is on the twelve, it doesn't mean that you can meet me at the entrance at twelve minutes past three. If you're one minute past three, you're grounded. Michael, what will happen if I am waiting at the entrance with Sean and the towels at three and then you come sauntering up at twelve minutes past three?"

"You mean when the big hand is on the twelve?" I asked.

She was silent.

"When the big hand is on the twelve it *will* be three o'clock," I said. I couldn't resist it. "When the little hand is on the three and the big hand is on the twelve, then . . ."

But my mother, throwing up her hands, was already walking

toward the mall, followed by Sean, his little legs jogging to keep up. Jenny scrutinized her watch.

"There's *two* twelves on this Swatch," she said.

"I know," I said. "Let's go."

•

Just inside the mall was the map of the mall. A wonderful map, lit up on a pedestal. It was usually surrounded by middle-aged ladies and teenage girls. You could tell by the way they stared—several seconds longer than necessary to determine the way to Famous Footwear or American Eagle—that they'd never had an opportunity to play a map-based computer game.

They were like the poor starving children in *A Christmas Carol*, staring through the glass at fabulous cakes and pies and dressed turkeys and hams. Except these oversize twentieth-century rich suburban urchins didn't even know what it was they wanted. They stood before the map of the mall radiating unfocused desire—desire to multiply their worlds, desire to multiply themselves in fantasy actions spangled across maps studded with words like "Diamond" and "Secret" and "Eagle." Eventually they sighed, charged with obscure desire, and headed out among the three-dimensional handbags and shoes.

That's why they put maps at the entrance to malls. Not to show people the shortest route to their destination—actually that's a drawback; the owners want people to get lost and wander among the window displays for as long as possible. They put the map there to create desire. To create the desire to escape. The desire to *get out*, to go *somewhere else* that every map elicits.

Studies have shown that a person exposed to a map immediately before shopping will spend 20 percent more.

I flicked a pitying look at the weekday afternoon crowd around the map and walked on. I knew where I was going. The map quarry. The computer-game store. *Babbage's*. They fit a hundred computer-game boxes in the display window. My eyes slid down the wonderful names and images. An unreality cascade. Antimatter falls.

And always, one box in particular precipitated from that flood. *Elite*. A black box, at the center a militaristic gold medal, like one of my grandfather's World War II medals. But instead of an eagle, the medal depicted the tufted sharp-eared skull of an alien bird of prey.

All I knew was that the game was about outer space. I'd first seen it at a store in Evanston. I knew I needed it right away. My parents had promised it to me for Christmas, but Christmas was half devoured by preparations for the move north, and left in its wake the amnesiac anti-present of a Nintendo system, complete with two controllers that looked like something adults would use for their jobs. They should be fucking *paying* me to do this shit, I thought all through January, monotonously stuffing Super Mario down chutes and up ladders. This is *child labor*, I thought as I smashed Mario's head against a brick again and again and again and again for gold coins.

One single coin a smash. Didn't anyone at Nintendo ever think to use a number? Like, hit this brick once and get thirty coins? Hit this brick and the number 30 floats up with the coins?

No, they made you see every coin as it popped up. They made you hit your head one time for one coin. In the industry they call this principle *making the player work for it*. The console designers ruthlessly apply the principle, turning their games into spiritual facsimiles of their own alienated labor. If you want a coin, smash your head against this brick. Want two coins? Smash smash. Want five? Smash smash smash smash smash.

Nintendo is for people who can't count past one, I thought. Nintendo is for people who don't know about numbers. They should flip the script. Instead of making games that work like jobs, they should apply the computer-game principle, the 490-points-of-damage principle, to jobs. Want to see what thirty years of work will get you? Press this button. Want to see what 490 years of work will get you? Press this button. That's enough time. Now let's talk about space. Here's a map.

Computer games distill the spiritual essence of time and space. Nintendo is spiritual cancer. By mid-January my sister and I tottered around like third-shift factory workers. To make matters worse, our parents were frantically unmaking the entire house around us, packing everything into a thousand cardboard boxes. Our life got literally taken apart while the smell of broken candy canes and microwaved macaroni went up around us, the sound of microwave beeps and packing tape, the sound of Mario smashing his head forty times against a brick to get forty pennies.

After this anti-Christmas came the actual move. I remember standing over the map of Chicagoland, following my mother's finger north until the dots of towns and the lines of features dwindled to nothing. Following my mother's finger still farther north through the useless blank map to the tiny microdot Mettawa. Then the redundant drive north through dwindling towns and features and a landscape that resembles what dead people see under their eyelids. And then the unpacking, amid the absolute alien horror of unfamiliar carpet and new toilets, amid five acres of snow, amid the sound of Mario smashing his head against a brick, amid the new silence of my parents. They stopped speaking to each other sometime after Valentine's Day.

To picture that first winter in Mettawa, imagine a cup. Imagine a cup fashioned to resemble the brick-squashed head of Super Mario, with his ears for handles. Now imagine the cup filled with the black milk of my parents' silence.

In early summer, after half the boxes were unpacked, my father disappeared. I heard a word I felt I had always known, a word that had slumbered, skeletal, inside every other word my parents had ever spoken. *Divorce.* My mother's brothers came over and moved the remaining boxes into the basement, where they remained for six years until a flood destroyed them.

My computer was in one of those boxes. Occasionally I'd go down into the box-ocean basement and pick a box at random. I'd open it and begin digging through the photo frames and tablecloths. Suddenly I'd touch a candelabra around which was wrapped one of my mother's long nerves and she would yell instantly from several stories above—*leave those goddamned boxes alone Michael I'm going to unpack them tomorrow you don't know where anything goes you're ruining everything.*

But when I couldn't sleep, I'd sneak down the carpeted stairs to the basement with a flashlight. I spent my midnights inspecting the detritus of my parents' marriage—a necklace my father had bought Mom, an old blanket I remembered from a photograph of them at a picnic. Then one night my fingers hit the pay dirt of computer plastic. The Commodore 64.

I lugged it up to the cavernous living room and set it up on a card table. But what is a computer without games? My allowance had been cut to nothing.

"There's plenty of bricks around here," Mom's eyes seemed to say, "go smash your head for pennies like you do in your fantasy."

"You've got Super Mario Brothers," her mouth would

actually say, "that's enough *escapism* for you. All this *escapism*. Just where do you think the money for more games is going to come from? Sometimes I think you kids are living in a fantasy world."

We were. That was the problem. I stared hopelessly at the cascading boxes in the Babbage's window in the mall. I watched the waterfall of computer games.

"The big hand is at the ten," said Jenny.

"Okay," I said. "I just need to go in here for a sec."

She rolled her eyes. Inside, the Babbage's employee looked down at me from the immaculate white counter.

"*Elite*," I said. "How much is it again?"

"Twenty-nine dollars and ninety-nine cents," he said. "Same as last week."

"Can I see the box?"

He handed it down to me. The back showed starmaps.

"Is it . . . good?" I asked.

He looked at me. Held out his hand. I reluctantly gave him the box.

"There's nothing like it," he said. He turned the box over in his hand, shook his head. "There'll probably never be anything like it again."

It's been twenty-seven years. So far he's right.

•

But I still had no money. Jenny dragged me out of the store. We ran, made it back to the entrance in the nick of time. Mom was standing there, giant towel-filled Sears bag in one hand, Sean's hand in the other. Staring at the map. You're supposed to look at the map *before* you go shopping, Mom. No one knows what happens if you stare at it afterwards.

"You kids are late," Mom said automatically when Jenny tugged her shirt.

"The big hand is on the first twelve," Jenny declared.

"We gotta hurry," Mom said. "The Rayburns are coming at four."

The Rayburns! Eric and Rich and their mother Ellen were coming. Our old friends from Evanston. We hadn't seen them in months. We hadn't seen *anyone* in months. Excitement jolted through the Suburban as Mom pulled out of the mall parking lot. Sensing the mood, she ejected Bette Midler and popped in the Bee Gees.

"Tragedy!" the Bee Gees yelled. "When you lose control and you got no soul it's tragedy!"

"Tragedy!" we all yelled.

Sean hugged his pet pillow. He had an old pillow he called Stinky as a pet.

"Tragedy!" he screamed, squeezing Stinky. "Tragedy! Got no soul! Tragedy!"

When the Suburban turned up our long driveway we were all red-faced from singing.

"Rayburns!" yelled Jenny.

Crazed grins reflected off the Suburban's interior surfaces. Other people! Other people! Mom looked at us through the rearview mirror. Looked at her own grinning red face. Realized that to be this excited at the prospect of seeing other human beings was unseemly.

"Okay, calm down, kids," she said. "Let's all just calm down now. The Rayburns will think we're crazy."

Crazy! Tragedy! Jenny and I wiped the grins off our faces and sat upright. Mom put the car in park and went inside to start getting dinner ready. We trooped in behind her. Where was Sean? Jenny turned back.

"Sean? Sean, where are you?"

He was standing outside the front door, looking out over the vast meadow toward the road, squeezing Stinky.

"Rayburns!" he shrieked.

"You're *embarrassing* us," Jenny hissed, grabbing his arm and pulling him inside.

Once inside, we contained ourselves. We contained ourselves to the point that we didn't even get up when we heard the Rayburns' wheels on the gravel. Mom sauntered into the living room, brushing flour from her jeans.

"It sounds like someone's here," she said in her best faux-calm voice.

We stood up and walked stiffly to the door. We controlled our overexcited limbs directly with our minds. Eric and Rich were coming up the walk when we emerged.

"Why are you guys walking like robots?" Rich asked.

"Oh, it's you," I said nonchalantly. "We thought it was the mailman."

"You come outside to see the mailman?"

"Their mailbox is at the end of the driveway," Rich observed. "I bet the mailman never comes up to the house."

"He does with special deliveries," I said.

Ellen interrupted these formalities by coming up the walk, carrying a tray of brownies.

"Where's your mom?" she called.

Mom appeared like magic in the doorway and rushed down to hug her. Ellen gingerly lifted the brownies with one arm away from the force of Mom's embrace.

"Great to see you too!" she said.

The tray wobbled above her, a meter registering the degree of Mom's social isolation. It began to shake wildly.

"Careful!" Ellen called, grabbing it with both hands.

Mom laughed awkwardly.

"We're just so glad you've come," she said.

•

"So how's it going," Eric said, slugging me in the arm play-fully. "So what do you got to do up here?"

"They've got Nintendo," Rich said, staring into the living room.

"Nintendo!" Eric yelled. "Super Mario?"

Jenny and I nodded miserably. They rushed to the TV and switched on the console, and all we heard until dinner was the sound of Mario's head smashing bricks.

After dinner Ellen and Mom wanted to talk in the living room, so they shooed us out. Jenny and Rich wandered off to the stables. Eric and I sat on the front step, looking out over the grassy acres.

"So you guys are pretty rich now, huh," Eric said. "Horses and shit, huh."

"I don't really like riding horses," I said.

"Your living room is as big as our house," he said flatly.

I didn't know what to say.

"How's Chip and John and the rest of the guys?" I asked.

"Chip's got a Nintendo," Eric said. "John doesn't."

We were silent for a while.

"Our basketball team's gonna be badass this year," Eric said.

"We can still hang out," I said.

He was silent. Picked up a pebble from the sidewalk, ex-amined it.

"It takes *forever* to get up here," he said.

Fuck this, I thought.

"Listen, I need some money, man," I told him in a low voice. He looked surprised.

"Don't give me that look," I said. "And don't say nothing about me being rich. I'd sell these goddamned horses for ten bucks apiece if I could. I don't have a penny."

"What about your mom?" Eric said.

I shook my head.

"She's broke too, everything goes on the credit cards. Plus, if she does get hold of a dollar, she checks her purse a hundred times a day to make sure it's still there."

"Well what do want me to do about it?" he said. "My allowance is ten bucks, and this week's is gone."

"Yeah, but your mom," I said fast. "Your mom wasn't carrying a purse when she came in here. So her purse has got to be in the car."

"You want to steal from my mom?"

"This is the first car we've had up here in a month," I said. "The last one was my grandma and she keeps her purse on her arm when she goes to the bathroom, for chrissakes. I'm sorry it's your mom and all but I need you to sit here and be the lookout while I go get thirty bucks out of her purse."

"No way," Eric said, standing up and crossing his arms.

"No way?" I said, standing up and balling my fists.

Eric took a step back.

"Chill out," he said. "What do you need thirty bucks for so bad? You already got Super Mario."

"Fuck Super Mario," I said.

"What do you need the money for?" he asked again.

I looked around desperately. My eyes hit the red bar of the sunset, lying over the black bar of the road. I turned my neck and my gaze hit the green bar of the meadow, the fleshy bars of the horses. Behind me lay the thick wooden bars of the house.

"I need to be somewhere else," I said.

"Let's go play Super Mario," Eric said soothingly.

I shook my head.

"That's too fake," I said.

"You've got a basketball court in back, let's go shoot some hoops."

I shook my head.

That's too real, I thought.

•

Eric wouldn't let me steal the money from his mother's purse. The Rayburns left before it was quite dark. My mother and sister and brother stood waving on the sidewalk as they drove away. Like idiots, I thought. I could see through the car's windows that none of the Rayburns were looking behind at the farewell spectacle on our lawn. Time to get real, I thought.

The next morning I approached my mother with a business proposition. I offered to clean out the horse stalls in exchange for money. She'd had to fire the groom the week before.

"Mexican labor is so *expensive*," she'd said.

Since then the stalls had been accumulating muck at a frightening rate. She had a demand and I had a supply. We bargained, her poverty grinding against mine until neither of us could move another cent. The final figure was $11.50 per week. All right. Three weeks till *Elite*.

Cleaning out horse stalls is no joke. It's real work. First, the labor of shoveling compacted layers of shit and straw into a wheelbarrow. Then wheeling the muck out of the stable, trundling it under the gigantic July sun, pushing it into the far field, and dumping it. Repeat.

The stables were in back, you couldn't see them from the road. Our big house concealed the sight of a child performing work no American would do for a wage no Mexican would consider. But that was just the social-justice view of the situation. I preferred to think of what I was doing as magic. Turning work into money is the fundamental alchemy of the capitalist system.

My first paying job was magical enough. But there was more. With each passage of the wheelbarrow from stable to shit-pile, the sun that shone pitilessly down on me, the sun that lit my mother's fantasy-reality, the sun of July 1988 . . . waned. Got smaller. Flaked away.

I don't mean the sun got literally smaller. Actually, I do mean that. But I don't mean that the sun got less bright and hot. Actually, no, I mean that too. The work gave me money, money gave me *Elite,* and *Elite* turned our giant sun into a distant star.

From deep enough in outer space the sun is just another star.

This is the fundamental truth of science. A space-based game like *Elite* brings the fundamental truth of science down on life, splitting it. After three weeks Mom drove me to the mall and we returned with the game. I put the disk in and turned on the computer.

We all know the sun is a star. But to *actually see* it? To see the sun as a star is a trick of the eyes. You have to trick your eyes to see the truth. *Elite* trained my eyes for the trick. Once your eyes can see the truth, nothing is the same.

When you first turn the game on, your eyes reel in shock. There are no surfaces in *Elite*. Planets, space stations, asteroids, and spaceships are transparent polygons through which you can always see the stars. For example, the small round disk—flared slightly at the edges—of your Mark III Cobra spacecraft. The thin kites of viper spacecraft, containing unscrupulous traders or even pirates. The monstrous ovals of Anaconda-class destroyers, the space navy of rich planets.

These ships are transparent in the game because of the *wireframe technology* the designers used to simulate 3-D surfaces on a computer screen. The name comes from the engineering practice of modeling objects in wire to show their shape. Sometimes engineers need to know how a shape fits with other shapes and don't have time to make a full solid model. Similarly, eighties PCs weren't powerful enough to generate the illusion of solid three-dimensional objects. But by rendering objects in the "wire" of white lines, the game could show a workable three dimensionality against the persistent 2-D of the starfield. The game map grew a phantom third dimension.

Here's how *Elite* works. The upper half of the computer screen shows the view out my spaceship's windscreen (or spacescreen). I see the black of space, the crosshairs of my laser weapon, the white pinpricks of stars, and the transparent polygons of space stations or spaceships.

The lower half of the computer screen shows my sensor. It's a kind of space radar. A red circular graph, with a thin green triangle at the top. The green triangle represents my frontal view, what I can see in the upper half of my screen. Various dots blink on the sensor. Friendly spacecraft or stations are represented by a benign white, enemies by red dots. To either side of the sensor are several bar graphs, representing my hull strength, laser power, and fuel.

My front view shows serene stars, moving slightly as I power toward a distant system. But now a red dot lights up at the far left edge of my sensor. I've got a bounty on my head, I need to be careful. Eyes on the sensor, I wheel left and speed forward, trying to bring the suspicious dot into the green triangle. Finally the dot brushes the edge of the triangle, and I look up at the top half of the screen to see a viper's transparent kite speeding over me. It's shrinking fast as it climbs, speeding away, and now it zips off the top of my screen.

Probably a pirate. The sensor shows it's still there. I hit W, wheeling up, thumb on space for speed—and there it is! Screaming straight at me, radiating white laser fire. And now my screen blanches, the bar representing my hull strength leaks color. Time for drastic action. I take my thumb off the space bar, my spaceship lurches to a sudden halt. I watch the pirate streak over me, and then watch his still-speeding dot shriek away on my sensor. Now the hunter becomes the prey. I swivel around, still stopped, tapping A and D until he's in the green.

And now I see him in my upper screen, like a tiny swollen star. I tap the keys until the crosshairs are directly on him. Put my thumb on space. I'm picking up speed. He's wriggling now. Tap A, tap D. Keep him in the crosshairs. Thumb on space. He wheels, I wheel. Now he's large enough to see stars through his angles.

I hit enter, my pulse lasers fire. He veers left, I follow, the white lines of my pulse laser heating his angles. He wriggles like a worm on a hook, but it's no good. I follow, heating his angles, heating his angles . . . Finally they shatter, spewing broken white lines and a handful of tiny transparent barrels. I scoop them up: ore, contraband narcotics, mining machinery. A nice haul.

It all happens in silence. Maybe some people got the sound to work on *Elite*, but with my Commodore 64 everything was silent. There were no surfaces. You can always see stars through every object, and it is always silent. That's outer space.

To live and die like that . . . listen! In reality there are no surfaces. Science knows this. Another fundamental truth. Point your microscope at a surface. Magnify down 100×. The surface begins to breathe. Molecules wriggle. Magnify down another 100×, the atoms are not touching. Magnify down another 100× and you can see space inside the atoms.

To live and die in a world without surfaces . . . And you can die. You will die. In *Elite* if you pilot your spaceship directly into a space station your ship will shatter, spewing broken white lines as "game over" crawls across the screen.

But you will see stars through the space station. A wireframe space station, spinning slowly, getting larger in your upper screen. That's what you see when you're headed toward death. Stars shine through the space station's missing surface. Hit the space bar. Keep getting closer. The lines of the space station's angles get larger. Keep your thumb on the space bar. Now you can no longer see the space station as a whole. You're too close. The white line of one of its angles bisects your screen. You see stars.

Keep your thumb on the space bar. The angle's gone. Stars. Nothing but stars. Only your sensor shows how close you are now; the giant white dot of the station almost covers the sensor's centerpoint. Keep going. You see stars through the space station. You see stars through the space station until the moment you shatter, and you will see stars through the space station after your ship shatters and "game over" dances across the starfield.

You see through the surfaces that kill you. They're not there. They trick your spaceship, true, they trick your body. But they're not really there.

It's the same down on Earth. When you're standing at the top of the Sears Tower you know that the sidewalk at the bottom is mostly composed of space—the space between the atoms, the space inside the atoms. The solid sidewalk surface you see is a trick. But it'll trick your body to death.

In life, the surfaces that trick your body also trick your eyes. *Elite* untricks your vision. So when you dive your spaceship into an empty wireframe model of a space station, your spaceship bursts apart. It feels uncanny. To get smashed to death on the surface of something you can see through feels strange. Your eyes literally look through your death. But it's just a side effect of the wireframe technology, right? It doesn't mean anything.

Right?

•

If I had been a different player, a better player, I might have missed the chance to look through my death. This uncanny experience wasn't supposed to happen. You were supposed to die under an enemy's lasers.

You get shot, you die. That's everyday life. No deep spiritual truth there. And for most players, that's how death came to them. The uncanny experience only happened to me when I dove into a space station. The experience of diving into the space station, the experience of seeing the angles grow larger and larger in my viewscreen, the experience of seeing the angles disappear, the experience of finding myself moving serenely through endless starry space until *Boom!* I shatter on empty space and die.

Uncanny. But it only happened when I dove into a space station. And you weren't *supposed* to dive into a space station.

But I did. I smashed myself to bits on transparent space stations again and again and again. I couldn't help it. I did it compulsively. Ten times a half hour. Twenty times an hour. In especially intense periods of play, I had the uncanny experience of seeing through my death every three minutes for two full hours.

I didn't mean to. I didn't want to. Oh God I don't want to. There's the space station. It's getting larger. Okay, now this time I'm not going to do it. Tap space gingerly. Please God don't let me do it. The angles get larger, stars swarm inside them. I'm not going to do it. Thumb on space. Please, no. The angles get larger, the stars swarm. Thumb *all the way down* on space. Oh God, I'm not going to do it, I'm not going to do it, I'm not going to do it *Boom!*

Repeat.

I wasn't having a psychotic episode. And I'm not one of those losers who refuse to play along with the game. Players who cruise around *Grand Theft Auto* deliberately running over innocent passersby and ignoring the legitimate missions. I'm not like those animals. I want to play the game. I want what the game gives me to want. I do not want to crash into the space station. And I tried not to do it. I tried *extremely hard*.

Let me explain. Let me back up for a second. Okay. You begin the game in outer space, with a small ship equipped with pulse lasers. The manual shows thirty-two different upgrades you can get for your ship. Two thirds of the giant manual is devoted to these upgrades, it's stuffed with them. Military-grade lasers. Fuel scoops. Hyperdrives. Shields. These are the objects the game has given you to want. I wanted them. Deeply. But to get them, I needed money.

That was no problem. I soon became adept at killing small trading craft, gathering up the barrels they spilled, accumulating credits. Of course, this put a bounty on my head, and sometimes the navy or pirates would lock onto my little Cobra. But eventually I got good at dodging the cops and killing the pirates. Eventually I was loaded. I had enough credits to get an upgrade. I wondered how tough those Anacondas would be with a military-grade laser burning a hole in their asses. Not so tough, I concluded. I had the desire for a military-grade laser. And I had the money.

But there was a problem. You could only purchase upgrades

in space stations. And to get into a space station, you had to dock. The dock was a rectangle set into the space station's face. The rectangle represented the station's docking bay. It was only slightly larger than my ship. So it was going to be a tight squeeze. By itself, that wouldn't have been a fatal problem.

But the space station was rotating.

The whole thing was spinning around like crazy. Why do space stations have to spin? I don't know, I think the spin helps to simulate gravity in the interior, like those terrible rides at amusement parks where they spin you around and you stick to the sides. I hope the people inside the space station enjoyed it. For me, the fact that the space station was spinning around like crazy meant that the rectangle I had to pilot my ship into was spinning around like crazy. In order to dock, I had to align my ship precisely with the station's rotation. I had to rapidly tap A and D as I accelerated to keep the rectangle straight so I could squeeze in.

I couldn't do it. It was simply impossible. Say the word "dock" to old *Elite* gamers and they'll smile and shake their head. They remember the incredible frustration of those docking maneuvers. Keeping that tiny rectangle precisely aligned while the station spun and you accelerated? Hard. Very hard.

But for me it was impossible. They say character is fate, and my fate has been shaped by two fundamental features: (1) an absolute love for computer games, and (2) absolutely no hand-eye coordination.

In fact, I possess the worst hand-eye coordination possible for an American to have without being eligible for disability payments. You wouldn't know it to look at me. It's not like I can't drive a car. I can. Maybe I'm not the best driver in the world, but I get around. I can get by in this world. I can use a phone. I can push a wheelbarrow.

But I could not dock in *Elite*. If I had a dollar for every time I watched the rectangle of the dock turn into a triangle and then into a line and then disappear entirely while the stars shone and I sailed into another uncanny death, I'd probably have two thousand dollars. Which I don't need. The things I really want cannot be bought with real-world money.

And it's not like I don't want things. I do. On a page near the back, for example, the *Elite* manual described one upgrade that looked especially attractive. A docking computer. "Take the stress out of docking," chirped the manual; "buy a docking computer and autopilot will take you in smooth every time."

But I didn't have a docking computer. I had the money, but I couldn't get to the store. The only thing that could save me was the docking computer, and the docking computer was on the other side of the dock.

So I spent 90 percent of my time in *Elite* seeing through my own death. Eventually it was 100 percent.

Even today, if I was to feel its contours, sense its uncanny dimensions, I'd recognize the feeling. The feeling of seeing through my own death. The feeling of being about to die on a fundamentally absent surface. I recognize it instantly. Like I can recognize my mother's face in a crowd.

And I've spotted it a few times out here. Not many. A few. On a highway at night, in a hotel room in Amsterdam. I've spotted it two times so far. It's out here.

•

"We have a Visitor," my mother intoned.

I furiously hit A, furiously hit D.

"Damn!" I yelled.

My spaceship spewed its angles across the stars. "Game over."

"I said, we have *a Visitor*," Mom repeated.

I looked away from *Elite*. Mom stood glowering by the door. I blinked, and stars flowed through her face. Blinked again. Her face closed.

"Why are you telling me this?" I asked.

Mom smiled mysteriously.

"She wants to talk to you," she said.

The Visitor's name was Annie Toole. Mom had met her at a divorce support group she'd attended briefly. Mom called her Annie, but she didn't think it appropriate for us kids to call her Annie.

"It's *Mrs.* Toole to you," she told us in preparation for Annie's first visit. "Wait, maybe it's *Ms.* Toole. Actually, wait, I don't even know if *Toole* is her married name. Maybe it's her maiden name. God. *Miss* Toole?"

When Mom was done preparing us for Annie's visit, two things were clear. We couldn't call the visitor Annie and we couldn't call her anything else. In different circumstances this might have created a problem. But since no other visitor ever came now, the name Visitor was enough to identify her.

"Where's Mom?" I'd ask, wearily trudging in from the stables.

"With the Visitor," Jenny would say.

We'd look at each other and roll our eyes. Mom and the Visitor spent most of their time talking in low voices in the kitchen. Phrases like "codependent relationship," "Jungian psychology," and "Gemini behavior" leaked out of the kitchen like weird smells. Sometimes they'd drive out together. We didn't know where they went. New Age bookstores probably, New Age coffee shops. We didn't care. I worked on *Elite*. Jenny read books. Sean talked to Stinky. We devoted ourselves to our separate disciplines for seeing through the fantasy world of our home life.

Now the Visitor had called me. Following Mom, I entered the kitchen and saw that the Visitor had her tarot cards spread over the table.

"Michael," my mom said sweetly. "Annie would like to read your cards."

Oh Jesus, I thought. Annie looked up at me. She was a plump blond woman in early middle age. She looked at me with concern.

"Your mother has been telling me of your troubles," she said.

Suddenly fear cut through my irritation. Did the Visitor know about my docking problems? How could she?

"What troubles?" I asked cautiously.

"You're lonely, Michael," she said. "You've moved away from all your friends and you're lonely."

Relief flooded through me.

"You're right," I said. "I guess I am pretty lonely."

"Of course you are, and the divorce! You poor abandoned kids, just the other day I said to your mom, Now, Barb . . ."

She droned on. Whew, I thought. I really couldn't have faced talking to this woman about my *Elite* problems.

". . . going to read your cards," Annie finished.

"What?" I said.

"Aren't you listening?" Mom asked sternly.

"It's okay, Barb," said Annie. "He doesn't have to do this if it makes him uncomfortable."

"Uh, sorry," I said. "I was thinking about . . . what did you just say?"

"You see?" Mom said to Annie. "You see what he's been like?"

Annie smiled patiently.

"Michael, I was just saying that you're going through a hard time," she said. "And I've gone through *very* hard times in my life, so I can tell. And I can tell you that sometimes when the present is very difficult, it helps to know what will happen in the future."

"The future?" I said.

She frowned.

"You don't have to do it if you don't want to," she snapped. "But that's no reason to make fun of something that saves people's lives."

She began to gather up her cards and put them back in their box.

"Wait," my mom pleaded. "Annie, wait. Please. He needs this so badly. He *wants* this so badly."

"No one has to do anything they're not comfortable with," Annie huffed.

My mother turned to me.

"Michael, you want Annie to read your cards, right?" she asked. "Trust me, you *want* to know. I've done it. And the future is wonderful! And even if *your* future is not so wonderful, even if there's challenges ahead, it's always better to know, right?"

"To know what?" I asked, bewildered.

"We don't need to decide what it is you'll know or not know right now," Annie said. "Let's just get the information from the cards. Then you can think about what you know and what you don't know."

She began dealing the cards out.

"Sit down, Michael," my mother whispered.

I sat on a wooden kitchen chair, across the table from Annie. Behind her I could see Jenny and Sean peeking through the doorway that led to the parlor.

Annie stopped dealing. She closed her eyes. She opened them. Then she gathered up the cards she'd just dealt. She shuffled. Sighed, stretched her hands out. For several seconds she remained motionless. Then she drew forth the cards slowly, one by one, arranging them deliberately, laying them across the surface of the table in weird patterns.

I saw that the backs of the cards were covered with runes.

There was a squeal from the doorway.

"*Jenny. And. Sean,*" my mother began. "*Get* your butts *away* from—"

"No," said Annie. "They can see. Let the children see."

Mom's frown turned upside down. She beckoned to them. They crept forward, Sean dragging Stinky behind him.

"What is it?" he asked, looking at the cards spread over the table.

"This is your brother's future," Annie said, turning to him and smiling. "Do you know what the future is, Sean?"

He stared back at her, mesmerized. He shook his head.

"I'll bet you do," said Annie. She swiveled to face him, took his little hands in hers. Stinky fell to the floor. "Do you know what it means when we say something is far away?"

"Yes," he said. He took his hands back. Picked up Stinky and squeezed.

"Tell me something that's far away."

"Evanston," he said.

Mom and Annie laughed.

"That's right!" said Annie. "Evanston is pretty far away. But what about something that's *really* far away. Like the moon! Have you seen the moon, Sean?"

He nodded slowly.

"Well, Sean," Annie continued. "Evanston isn't really that far away, but we can't see it from here. The moon is *really* far away, but we *can* see it from here. Every night, if it's clear we can see it. Right?"

Sean nodded.

"The moon is so far away," she said. "People like you and me, who don't have fancy spaceships, we can't even get there."

"Michael has a spaceship," Sean said.

"Shut up, Sean!" I growled.

But Annie ignored this interruption.

"The future is just like the moon, Sean," she continued. "Now, we can see some of the moon's features with our naked eyes. But we can't see them very well. So what do we do if we want to see the moon better?"

Sean looked absolutely befuddled.

"A telescope!" Annie shouted. "If something is too far away to visit, we use a telescope to see it. Sean, these cards are a kind of telescope for seeing the future!"

She beamed at him triumphantly.

"The future?" Sean said.

"You know, like Christmas," said Annie. "Christmas is in the future."

"*You can see Christmas?*" Sean breathed, his eyes widening.

"Maybe the little ones should wait in the other room," Annie said, turning to Mom.

"You heard her," Mom said.

"I'm not little," Jenny protested.

"Out!"

When they were gone, Annie gave me a little smile. Mom let out a squeal of delight.

"This is so exciting!" she said. "Oh, Michael, what do you think the cards will say?"

"Hush, Barb," said Annie. "I need silence."

She began to turn the cards over.

A knight.

A tower.

A sword.

The cards showed an artist's conception of the things in *The Bard's Tale II*.

"I've seen these pictures before," I said.

But my mom and Annie were staring at the cards, trans-fixed.

"Did you do it right?" Mom whispered.

"I did it just like I always do," Annie whispered back.

"Shit," Mom said.

"I've never seen anything as bad as this," Annie whispered. "Not even Craig's cards were like this. Not even close."

"I've seen these pictures before," I said more loudly.

"Oh, honey," Annie said, looking up at me with vast pity.

"Maybe the cards are wrong," said Mom quickly. "Maybe they're just totally wrong!"

•

When the Visitor left, Mom took me aside and told me that the cards had predicted that something terrible would happen to me exactly ten years later. And you know what? It turned out the cards were right. Something terrible did happen. July 1998. It was in a hotel room in Amsterdam. The bag of white powder dropped from my fingers, I fell back on the bed. My girlfriend's scream froze in my ears.

And when the stars came through the transparent hotel room walls, I recognized the feeling. I recognized it from *Elite*.

Fuck tarot cards. It's not like they don't work, though. I know they work, at least sometimes. But fuck tarot cards any-way. It's like standing in your backyard looking through a tele-scope. Sure, you can see something. But if you really want to find out what's on the moon, you need a spaceship.

6.

Pirates!

Spaceships are useful for exploring the boundaries of existence. Like the future. Or the way matter warps under intense pressure. Or aliens. But if you really want to find out what *this* world is all about, you need a pirate ship.

Before we moved away from Evanston, back when Eric and I were still close, Ellen used to take me with them to their summer place in Michigan. It was right on the big lake. Eric and I would paddle around near the shore on his canoe. We'd look out at the yachts passing on the horizon.

"We could be pirates," he said.

He stuck his bowie knife into the wooden bench of the canoe. I pictured us paddling up to the side of one of the giant yachts.

"We'd have the element of surprise," I said.

"We could say we were lost," he said.

"They'd toss a rope ladder down," I said.

"I'd go up first."

"I'd go up second."

"You'd have the knife," he began.

"In my teeth," I finished.

We laughed. The canoe bobbed in the mild summer waves. Eric said, "And then what would we do?"

"Well," I said, "we'd make the yacht people our slaves. Then we'd sell all their silverware and shit."

"And use it to get a machine gun," Eric said. "And paint a skull on the side of the yacht."

"No more element of surprise," I said.

"You don't need surprise when you've got a machine gun," he pointed out.

"I bet those rich people on those yachts would *still* be surprised," I said. "They'd be sipping mixed drinks watching our boat coming and thinking, *Someone's playing a joke.*"

"They'd see the slaves on the deck," Eric pointed out.

"Yeah, their old friends from the country club, Polo rags wrapped around their waists."

"Chains wrapped around their legs," said Eric.

"But they *still* wouldn't get it," I said. "They'd be sitting on their yacht sipping mixed drinks, like, *Is someone filming a movie?*"

"They'd be, like, *That sure looks like George.*"

"In those rags," I said.

"With those chains," said Eric.

"They'd be, like, *Jesus! Is that crap on George's pants?*"

"*Oh my God, it looks like blood!*"

"Machine gun time," I sang out.

We laughed. The canoe rocked. The yachts passed to and fro on the horizon. Eric said, "Then what?"

"We'd sell the silverware," I said. "We'd sell the liquor. We'd sell the slaves."

"Real money," he said.

"Yeah," I said. "And we could, like, buy those cherries that grow here, the ones that my mom and everyone in Evanston go crazy for? We could bring it over to the other side in our pirate ship. Sell that shit."

"More money," said Eric.

We fell silent. He said, "Then what?"

"Then we're in the game," I said. "Then we're buying and selling. Take the money from selling the cherries and buy candy. Take the money from selling the candy and buy cars. Take the money from selling the cars and buy gold. Sell the gold. Buy airplanes."

I shook my head. "You can do that shit forever."

"You can do it forever," Eric agreed.

We fell silent, thinking.

"And never get bored?" Eric asked.

"I mean," I said, "isn't that the kind of thing that Mr. Halpern does?"

Mr. Halpern was the rich father of a kid who went to our school. He was a banker or something.

"That guy never looks bored," Eric said. "Buying and selling, huh."

His brow furrowed. "Hey, isn't that what our dads do? Buy and sell shit?"

I thought about it.

"Yeah, I guess that's what it comes down to," I said.

"Isn't that what everyone does?" Eric said. "All the adults, I mean?"

"Except the cops," I pointed out.

"Except the cops," Eric agreed.

"And the teachers," I said.

"Except for the cops and the teachers," he agreed. "But everyone else. Basically everyone else?"

"Yeah," I said.

Eric laughed.

"I guess that's the one thing our dads actually do that they make a computer game about," he said. "I guess that's the one cool thing they do."

"They make a computer game about what our dads do?" I asked.

"Yeah," said Eric. "It's called *Pirates!*"

•

I got *Pirates!* ASAP. It wasn't a game of mindless killing, sacking, and looting. Actually, it was mostly about trading. Say you capture a merchant ship with a cargo of cotton. So now you and your money-hungry crew have a bunch of cotton. You don't want cotton, you want gold. What do you do with the cotton? If you're smart, you take it to Barbados and sell it. Then, if you're really smart, you take the money and use it to buy rum. Take it to Caracas and sell it at a profit. Repeat. That's how you get ahead. That's how you win. Buying and selling.

Eric exaggerated, though. Our dads didn't do the same kind of thing as the pirates in the game. Not at all. As far as I could tell, Dad spent most of his time at work talking. Pirates don't talk much. In *Pirates!*, talking is pretty much kept to a minimum. Not at Dad's office. He brought me to his office once. It seemed like the phone never stopped ringing. His desk was covered with pictures of him smiling with people, shaking hands with people. People kept coming in and out of the office. More smiling, more talking. There was some buying and selling going on somewhere in there. I heard a couple of numbers mentioned. But they were buried under a mountain of talking and smiling. Offices are like that.

So Eric was wrong, I concluded. *Pirates!* didn't show us

what our dads did in their offices. It showed us what they could be doing. What they should be doing. *Pirates!* showed us what those offices could be like.

Imagine a wind from paradise, blowing through the offices. It blows the smiling and talking away. All that's left is a sea of numbers. And a map. Welcome to *Pirates!* Sugar goes for 40 over here, 80 over there. Buy the sugar here, put it in the pirate ship, and go sell it over there. Rum goes for 30 over there, 60 over here. Buy it there, sell it here. No problem. Most of the people you meet in *Pirates!* are cool. They know the deal. There's not much to say. Most of them them just want to know your numbers. Most of them you can deal with.

But sometimes you get one of these smiler-and-talkers. Sometimes, even in *Pirates!*, you get one of these office types. Nine times out of ten, when someone comes up to you in *Pirates!* and wants to talk, it's trouble. It's the cops. They've got a whole lot of questions. A whole lot of rules. Where'd you get that cotton? Where's your license to sell this stuff?

That's when you need your sword. That's when you need your cannon. That's when you need your pistols. That's where the killing, sacking, and looting comes in.

But it's not mindless killing, sacking, and looting. It's *Pirates!*, not *Maniacs!* People call pirates psychopaths, but it's not true. They're businessmen. They're the ultimate businessmen. They see that our world is inefficient. Of course most businessmen see this, but pirates see it clearly. To a pirate, our world is *terribly* inefficient. All this talking. All this hanging around on the phone, the Internet, the office, talking, talking, talking. Jesus. These people only stop talking long enough to smile. They only smile long enough to think of something to say. It's enough to drive you out of your mind.

And it's bad for business. Numbers are shy. They go into hiding when people start talking. You can't hear the numbers move through all that talking. For example. Here's some smiling guy with his hand out. His numbers are weak. They're puny. They're minor. But already you can't hear them. Already you've forgotten. All you can hear is this guy and his flood of meaningless words.

And it gets to you. You can't help it. You feel a *smile* spreading over your face. The smile of the forgetfulness of numbers. It's like a hole in your face. Your brains leak out. Look around. Everyone in the office has one. Crescent-shaped face holes, and they're spreading. They're contagious. This guy in front of you has had one for twenty years. His hole is so wide and so old that you can see outer space in it. You can see stars in it.

Who's the psychopath? Pirates are about efficiency. Like all businessmen. Pirates are like all businessmen except they love efficiency more than all businessmen. They love efficiency more than they love businessmen. They have love. They have courage. They have the *courage* to do what their *love* tells them. Pirates work to make the world safe for numbers. They work to stop the talking.

Killing, sacking, looting. Violence is a wind from paradise. It clears away the babble. When the wind recedes, the numbers poke their heads out. They begin to move. They start their transformations. Sugar turns into number which turns into rum which turns into number which turns into wood which turns into number which turns into towns, ships, bridges. Numbers rich with future flow through an ocean. The ocean is shaped like the Caribbean.

When numbers go sailing, they fly the skull and crossbones.

●

CHAPTER 5

The Common Man

I'd gotten the game in Evanston, a couple of months before we moved to Mettawa. The game got lost in the move. Then there was no money. And then, when I learned to turn work into money, there was *Elite*. I'll always be grateful for what *Elite* showed me. But when you're thirteen you can only take so much seeing through your own death. I stood alone at the end of the summer, with a heart full of pulverized spaceship angles.

You could say I was tired of space, that I was tired of endlessness. The truth is that I needed a different kind of endlessness. I began to crave *Pirates!*

It's not always easy to know when you're ready for a new game. It's like changing a habit. Let me explain. Most of what computer games do they do through habit. Computer games know that something that happens only once doesn't mean much to humans. Once-in-a-lifetime events tend to bounce off us. We're pretty hardened against rare occurrences. Blame evolution. If we changed our whole setup in response to every single new stimulus that came along, we'd never have gotten out of the swamps. Something that happens ten times, a hundred times, a thousand times. That kind of thing gets through to us. That kind of thing matters. Something that happens ten thousand times? It penetrates our innermost layer. It becomes part of us.

And that's how computer games work. Everything that happens in a computer game happens ten thousand times. Because computer games mimic habit, they get through to us. They teach us about the big things in a way nothing else can. They teach us about death, about character, about fate, about action and identity. They turn insights into habits. The habits bore through our defenses. Computer games reach us.

And conversely. If an insight can't be made into a computer game, it can't reach us. It's not for us. It's not real. It's not true. A lot of smart people have spent the past quarter century trying to turn any and every idea into a computer game. So there's a good chance that all possible true ideas are already contained in the history of computer games. That the history of computer games is also a philosophical encyclopedia containing every important truth available to our species.

That's my opinion, anyway. You think I wrote a book about computer games for fun? If I want fun, I'll play a computer game.

But the same thing that makes WAD [space] such an effective pirate ship for exploring the seas of truth also makes it hard to know when you need a new computer game. I mean, the game has gotten into you. It's just what you do. You don't think about whether or not you want to do it. You do it. So it can be hard to know when a game has worn itself out in you.

Sometimes, of course, you'll just get bored. The habit will no longer put you in touch with life-giving fun, with soul-sustaining truth. It'll run dry. It'll start to feel like Nintendo. Like unpaid work. When that happens, it's obvious. Time for a new game.

Sometimes, though, it's not so obvious. Sometimes you have to listen deep down into yourself. Listen. You're not bored. The game is still fun. It's still pretty fun. But if you listen deep down into yourself, down into the depths where WAD [space] is busy rearranging your senses . . . Wait. There's something wrong.

What is it? It's hard to put your finger on. Okay. Play like a doctor. Something feels wrong. What does it feel like, exactly?

I know what it feels like for me. But maybe it feels different for other players. I've done a little research.

Q. What makes you decide to stop playing a certain game?

A. I don't know. I just get bored.

Q. But do you ever decide to stop playing a game when you're not bored with it?

A. Sometimes, I guess. Sure. Sometimes.

Q. What makes you decide to stop?

A. I don't know. I just get, I don't know. I get tired of it?

Q. Tired of it. But not bored?

A. I guess.

Q. What does that feel like?

A. I don't know! Jesus, Mike. It's just a game, okay?

When it comes to probing questions about their intimate life as computer-game players, most people don't have much to say. They've never thought about it. Or they've repressed it. Or they've forgotten. Or they're embarrassed. Society has convinced them that computer games are a trivial pastime and there's no reason to think about them. So when I talk about the feeling that lets me know I've played a game too long, I can only speak for myself. Here goes.

When I've been playing a game for too long, I feel despair.

I don't know where it comes from. Maybe WAD [space] drilled too far down in me. Like a drill in the earth. First it breaks through the crust. It breaks through to coal. Good. Then it breaks through the coal to discover gold. Better. Then to diamonds. Now the game's really getting good.

But the drill-game keeps going. It keeps drilling down into me. It starts hitting empty levels.

Despair hisses up through the drill hole.

Playing *Elite* that August, I wasn't bored. The space station docking death was frustrating, of course, terribly frustrating. But there was still plenty to do. Plenty of vipers to hunt down. Plenty of Anacondas to dodge. It was still fun.

I was sitting at the computer, staring at the screen. I'd been playing for maybe an hour. Slow static snowed down on my nerves. Nothing to worry about. Just normal WAD [space]

buildup. Like soap scum in your tub. Nothing that couldn't
be scrubbed out with a little break, a vigorous walk around
the pastures.

But then, suddenly, there was something else. A new feeling. It happened while I was chasing a viper. Following his red
dot on the sensor until it swung into the green triangle and
then up on my viewscreen. I was in the zone. My fingers
floated across WAD [space]. Moving by themselves. Going
on pure habit. Beautiful. My bad coordination, history. My
system rewired by gamehabit. I locked on the viper and fired.

And caught a glimpse of the afternoon sun on the floor-
boards out of the corner of my eye.

And thought out of the corner of my mind, *nothing matters, I don't care about anything anymore.*

It was gone in a flash. I was absorbed again, watching the
viper's angles disintegrate under my laser fire.

But the very next day I put *Elite* back in its box. Time for a
different game. I searched frantically for days through the sea
of boxes in the basement for the copy of *Pirates!* I'd gotten in
Evanston. No luck. But the game was on discount at Babbage's. I went back to work in Mom's stables.

•

The next week I had it. The game is set in the Caribbean. The
Spanish Main. At the beginning of the game you get to choose
whether you want to be Spanish, English, French, or Dutch.
Then you get to decide whether you want the game to start in
1580, 1620, 1640, or 1680.

Then there's a short video sequence—a "cut scene"—
showing you as an urchin starving under the corrupt government of the Old World. You travel to the New World to make
your fortune. Along the way the evil captain gets overthrown

by the crew, and they elect you leader. Pirate is your name. Living free is your game.

And now it starts. The screen shows a blue map of ocean. In the center there's a tiny picture of a ship. That's you. Your sails show which way the wind is blowing. You can move fast with the wind, or slowly tack against it.

There's no plot. There's no goal. There's no story. There's just a world. A sea surrounded by strips of Central and South America, dotted with a few islands.

Pirates! is what's known as a "sandbox" game. Games like *Wolfenstein* or *Suspended* have goals. They have narrative. The game wants you to go from point A to point B. From the beginning, where Hitler is alive, to the end, where Hitler is dead. You move your avatar, but you don't have a whole lot of choice about where to move it. There's a Nazi at the end of that corridor. Kill him. There's a door behind him. Open it. A stairway. Go up.

In *Pirates!*, there's just an open world. Total freedom of choice. You can sail around and explore. You can visit Jamaica. You can visit Maracaibo. You can spend the whole game trading sugar and rum. You don't have to kill, burn, and loot. Being a pirate isn't about violence. It's about freedom. You can do whatever you want.

Someone is trying to stop you from doing whatever you want. The Government. Spain is the only real government on the Spanish Main. Spain is the prime generator of rules and talk. They don't believe in free trade. They don't like to see you sailing around. They've got their eye on you.

Here I am. I've just sold a load of sugar to a black market merchant. I'm minding my own business. Here comes a Spanish war galleon with sixty guns. Someone tipped him off. Someone talked. If he catches me, I'll do years in prison. My crew: shark bait. My gold will fill government coffers.

So I hit his giant slow ass with a point-blank twenty-gun volley from my speedy barque. Then I catch the wind and zip around his other side, slam him again while he's turning. This slow government stooge looks like Curly and I'm Moe. Soon he's full of holes and on fire and sinking and I take his silverware and his cannons and I put him in chains and give his crew a chance to live free or die.

That right there is a story. The game designers didn't make it up. It just happened. That story pulled itself up by its own bootstraps. That's how stories are born in *Pirates!* Narrative flowers from your choices. Narrative flowers from the encounter between freedom and government.

Okay. Now I've got a lot of guns. I've recruited crew members from all the taverns, jails, and alleys of the Spanish Main. We number in the thousands. Panama lies before us. The gigantic fort looms out of the government land. 2-D. On one side, brick and metal. On the other side, freedom.

We blast the bottom of the fort until it flips over. Until it opens up. Freedom pours out. Gold-colored freedom. It looks like money. It is money. A lot of money. Money is movement. Money is force. Money turns necessity into choice. No into yes. Money turns boundaries into doors. Talking into doing. Money turns smiles into the thing that smiles stand for.

If you pour enough money into a story, it bursts. Pure fun shines in the storyburst. There's a poem by the Portuguese poet Fernando Pessoa that captures what I'm trying to say here. Here's my favorite line:

Ah, pirates, pirates, pirates!

I forget the rest. The basic idea is clear enough. I loved *Pirates!*, and I don't mean maybe. The real-world application followed swiftly. School started. Eighth grade. Catholic school, of course. St. Joe's. *Pirates!* was going to teach me how to solve my school problems. I had major school problems. We'd moved in the middle of the previous school year, and what with the divorce and no computer games and all that new space and painful breaks with old friends, my social transition had been a little rocky. The first day at lunch I picked a table at random and sat down. It turned out to be the "smart kids'" table. My introduction to their little circle set the tone.

"I'm Kurt," said one faintly goofy looking kid with a blond buzz cut. "I'm going to be a chemist."

Two smirking kids walked by the table. One of them slammed into Kurt's chair.

"Sorry, Beef," he said. "It was an accident."

"Yeah, Beef," said the other.

"I'm sorry again, Beef."

"It's okay," Kurt muttered.

"No, Beef. I'm really sorry, Beef. Okay, Beef?"

When they'd left, Kurt looked at me and smiled.

"Now, where were we," he said, "before we were so rudely interrupted?"

"Why did they call you Beef?" I asked.

"Beef?" he said, looking puzzled. "Did they call me that? I guess I didn't hear. I have no idea why they'd call me that."

Ralph, the smart kids' table's future lawyer, nudged me.

"They call him Beef because one time he farted during assembly and it was so bad Mrs. Dennison gave him a detention."

"Oh, don't drag up ancient history," said Kurt, rolling his eyes.

"It was the only time in the history of the school that someone's been given a detention for farting," Ralph said primly.

"Shut up, Ralph," said Kurt.

"I asked my father and he said he didn't think it was legal for someone to be given a detention for farting."

"That's enough," said Kurt.

"But," Ralph continued, "my father did say that if it was an especially foul and stinky fart, a detention might be appropriate. A detention would be appropriate for a *disruptive* fart."

"I'm warning you," said Kurt.

"Beef said he didn't do it on purpose, and Dennison believed him," said Ralph. "She gave him the detention anyway. Usually a detention is for something you *do*. Not for something you *are*. My father says a fart like Beef's blurs the line."

"I'm double warning you," said Kurt.

"Mike, have your parents ever used an expression along the lines of, *I'm mad at you for what you did, but I love you for who you are?*"

"Sure," I said.

"Well, Beef is the kind of person that the school had to punish both for what he did and for what he is. My father thinks that in this case, the school's actions were appropriate."

"Shut the hell up, Ralph," said Kurt.

"No, *you* shut up, Beef," Ralph replied. "And quit trying to get the new kid to call you Kurt."

These people are scum, I thought. I picked the wrong table.

But in seventh grade, first impressions are durable. And the sight of me engaged in deep conversation with Beef and Ralph wasn't soon forgotten or forgiven in the halls of St. Joe's. The fact that I wore glasses and was a spectacularly untalented athlete didn't help. My situation was brought vividly home to me by an exchange in computer class with the prettiest girl in school, Allison K. It was two kids to a computer. We sat next to each other.

"This semester we are studying *Oregon Trail*," the nun at the head of the class intoned. "When you have satisfactorily completed *Oregon Trail*, you may begin *Where in the World Is Carmen Sandiego?*"

She paused. Took a deep breath. "Only those students who have completed *Oregon Trail* to my satisfaction will be allowed to progress to *Where in the World Is Carmen Sandiego?*"

This is my education, I thought. Catholic school in a semi-urban place like Evanston was bad enough, I thought. Out here in the boonies they're operating beyond any decency or restraint. Now the nun had really worked herself up. She was screaming.

"There is a severe penalty," the nun screamed, "for progressing to *Where in the World Is Carmen Sandiego?* without FULL and SATISFACTORY completion of ALL the MANY CHALLENGES you will face in *Oregon Trail* as you trek across a desolate and dangerous frontier in your COVERED WAGON on your way to Oregon to begin a NEW LIFE WITH YOUR FAMILY. The PENALTY for progressing to *Where in the World Is Carmen Sandiego?* without FULL completion of *Oregon Trail* is—"

The nun was loud, but the sight of Allison six inches away from me was louder.

"I'm Mike," I whispered, sticking my hand out.

She regarded it distastefully.

"I know you," she whispered. "You're Beef's friend."

"ALLISON!" boomed the nun. "Shall I leave the room so you can continue your conversation?"

"It's not my fault," she said. "*Beef's friend* is bothering me."

Every eye turned to me. Every mind fixed me. *Beef's friend*.

My hopes for social distinction in my new school shriveled.

Then came summer, and child labor, and *Elite*, and *Pirates!*
Summer hardened me. *Elite* beat me down, and *Pirates!* built
me back up. Into a machine. A monster. I faced September and
the new school year with a feeling that the game was about to
change.

This is going to be my breakthrough year, I thought to myself, checking out my new shirt in the mirror. Operation: Shut
down these teachers and their bullshit by any means necessary. Operation: Let these other kids know I run things around
here. Operation: Wipe that smile off your face. Operation:
This is the deal, there's nothing to talk about. Operation: Act
like a pirate and get money.

My new attitude found a congenial environment in the St.
Joseph's eighth-grade class of 1988–89. The first day of school,
Principal Dennison visited us personally. I'd never seen her
before. But I knew she was government before she opened
her mouth. I knew it by the look on her face as she regarded
us. The higher-ups in the Catholic school world are distin-
guished from the rank-and-file teachers by the quality of their
hatred for the students. The average teacher's hate runs hot.
Principal Dennison's hatred was ice cold.

"We had some serious discipline problems last year," she
began. "I hesitate to share with you the considered opinion
of the faculty that your class is the worst we've ever seen. My
hesitation does not spring from my regard for the delicacy
of your feelings. Indeed, the events of last winter convince
me you have none. No, my fear is rather that you will tend to
view this shameful distinction as a badge of honor."

She paused, looked around.

"I see from your faces that my fear is justified," she said.
"Very well. You want to be criminals. We will be punishers."

She turned on her heels and walked out the door. Mr. Filleto
shot a warning glance at us, then rushed out after her.

The classroom, temporarily devoid of teachers.

The ceiling fan, spinning slowly in the September heat.

Tim L., standing up, picking up a chair, throwing it directly overhead.

The fan cracks, spits out wood. The chair drops in pieces. The class roars with anarchic laughter. Mr. Filleto and Principal Dennison storm in. His cheeks go red. Her color recedes further into absolute whiteness.

"Who in God's name is responsible for this flagrant act of vandalism?" he shouted.

"A soul capable of such an act cannot be hidden," Dennison said softly.

"I didn't do it!" Beef shouted. "I didn't do it!"

The kid next to me ducked down, made a loud fart noise by blowing on his arm. The class bloomed with laughter. Dennison pointed a bony finger at Beef.

"Detention," she said.

The class roared like the sea. Late summer sunlight hit the small faces, turning them gold.

•

Is an eighth-grade classroom more like an office or a pirate ship? We were going to find out. Maybe you think this is a trivial question. Okay. Let me put this in perspective for you.

It's the fall of 1988. The last days of the Cold War. Communism is basically over. The future belongs to capitalism but suddenly no one knows what that means anymore. Capitalism. Buying and selling. Selling and buying. Is buying and selling more like an office building or more like a pirate ship? The choice of our generation. Here's the capitalism-as-piracy scenario. Imagine buyers and sellers crowding the deck of a ship. They're yelling.

"Walk the plank! Walk the plank!"

Here comes a house.

"Walk the plank! Walk the plank!"

The house walks to the end of the plank and closes its eyes and holds its nose and *jumps* into the ocean of money. It dissolves and turns into a number. The buyers and sellers cheer. Here comes a doctor.

"Walk the plank! Walk the plank!"

The doctor walks to the end of the plank. He closes his eyes and holds his nose and *jumps* into the ocean of money. Dissolves and turns into a number. The pirates cheer.

Anything can walk the plank. Everything will walk the plank. Food. Sex. Guns. Education. Religion. Friendship. Flowers. Over the plank! Into the ocean of money, where food sex guns education flowers move and flow and combine and recombine. The numbers curl up and transform and shoot out of the sea in rockets and rain down in showers—$20,000! $38! $149! $354,000! The pirates don't smile, they laugh. The pirates don't talk, they make you walk the plank.

Is capitalism more like a pirate ship or an office building? To find out what the capitalism-as-office-building scenario is like, just look around you. And don't tell me you work from home. I work from home. It just means you've turned your house into an office building.

Okay. Just some historical background on our situation in the St. Joe's eighth-grade class of 1989 as we looked around and wondered whether we were in an office building or a pirate ship. Whether the government ran things or whether the pirates did. After Mr. Filleto got done screaming at us and the bell rang and we leaped out of our chairs, I made my way over to Tim L.

"Hey," I whispered.

"What?"

"I just want you to know that I think you did the right thing," I whispered.

He gave me a blank look.

"I mean when you threw that chair up and broke the ceiling fan," I said earnestly. "I just wanted to tell you that I think that was the right thing to do."

Tim stared at me. Then he relaxed, held up his hand.

"High five," he said.

"Yes," I said. "Hey."

"What?"

"We gotta do something."

"Yeah," said Tim.

"We gotta do something big," I said.

"What's your plan?"

"I'm working on it," I said.

"What's your name?" he asked.

"I'm Mike," I said.

That afternoon on the bus ride home I thought about the situation. The minute that chair had hit that ceiling fan, I'd been converted. This is what I was looking for, I thought. This will solve my school problems, I thought. Now I saw the truth. My social problems at school were so deep that solving them required solving the more basic problem of school itself. And I couldn't do that alone. I had to be part of something bigger than me. I had to be part of a *movement*. Tim started the movement with that chair. A chair in the air. That chair was our Bastille.

The *movement* was anarchy. Good. A good start. Broken furniture. Kids yelling out dirty words in the middle of English class. Writing on the walls with permanent marker. Good. But it also made me nervous. The problem with anarchy is, it's unfocused. Like a cloud of smoke. Like a riot.

I needed a riot that lasts. I needed a fire that keeps smoking.

If this was a computer game, I thought, we could just add some numbers. I'd learned *The Bard's Tale II* lesson. The *D&D* lesson. You've got a nice fantasy. Okay. You're a knight killing orcs in a castle. All right. It's a nice daydream. Daydreams dissolve. Want it to last? Put in some numbers. Roll some dice. Numbers build a foundation under your fantasy. They make it last.

I got home, turning the problem over in my head as I sat down, turned on *Pirates!,* and set my fingers free on WAD [space]. The war galleons were chasing me. I had a crew of sugar I needed to unload. Then I could beef up on cannon and take on the Spanish and *wait*!

It came to me. The way to put some numbers under our real-life schoolhouse anarchic fantasy. Buying and selling! Buying and selling is how numbers get into real life.

I had a vision of the whole school as a black market. Every kid furiously absorbed in trading, buying, selling. The teachers totally mystified. They've lost control. Now the kids have their own economy. Now the kids are making their own money. The movement would be unstoppable. Unkillable. Buying and selling was irresistible. Even the kids who wouldn't go for anarchy would go for that. Even Beef, who would rather eat his own tongue than say "fuck," even he couldn't turn down the opportunity to make a little cash between classes.

Buying and selling was a virus that would eat the face of authority.

But we needed something to buy and sell. What? We had nothing. All we had were the pieces of whatever we could break. Broken chair bits. Broken chalk. Broken pens. Plus whatever our moms put into our lunch bags. Basically nothing. The government kept us down by keeping all salable goods far away from us. This to me was proof that I was on the right track. That the one thing Dennison most feared was that we'd turn the school into a black market, a Caribbean sea, circa 1620. Every classroom a pirate ship. This was her nightmare. I was sure of it. So it became my dream.

But it was just a dream. How to get it started? You had to have money so you could buy things to sell. But you had to have things to sell to get the money to buy.

There had to be a solution. I thought about how it worked in *Pirates!* How had I gotten that first load of cotton? Oh yeah. That's right.

I stole it.

•

At St. Joe's we had recess on a big field across the street from the school/church complex. You went there if you wanted to play football during recess. The field was surrounded on three sides by busy streets. Beyond the busy streets were residential areas. Quiet houses. The owners were probably at work during the day, but still. It didn't even occur to me. Not at age thirteen. Not yet. Breaking and entering was still beyond my imagination. I hadn't yet learned to see people's *very houses* as pirate ships.

So I saw no possibilities on the football field. The football field was no good.

But if you wanted to play basketball, then you went to the dilapidated basketball court on the side of the school. The court was surrounded by a high chain-link fence. Directly across the street from the court was a drugstore. No breaking and entering necessary. The stuff was just laid out waiting to be stolen. The drugstore was the merchant ship we'd loot to get the start-up goods for our numbers game.

I had the plan. Now I just had to sell it to my new friend Tim. I could kind of tell Tim didn't play computer games. It would have been counterproductive to tell him about the stuff I'd learned from *The Bard's Tale II* and *Pirates!* I resolved to break it down to him in stages.

I made my move during lunch. Got up from the friends-of-Beef table and walked boldly over to the cool kids' table. A phalanx of popular faces lined each side. I was nervous, but committed. I had a legitimate reason for this unprecedented act of social border crossing. I had a plan. Tim had his back to me. I tapped him on the shoulder.

"Hey, Tim," I said.

He turned around and looked at me like he'd never seen me before. The other cool kids' faces wavered between bemused and angry. I had to act fast.

"Hey," I said, "I got a plan."

Comprehension suddenly washed over him.

"Oh yeah. Mike. From yesterday."

The elaborate pretense, rigorously practiced by the popular kids, of not knowing the names of any dork besides Beef was a little much. The eighth-grade class only had thirty kids, for crissakes. But I let it slide.

"Yeah, right," I said. "Listen."

"What?"

"You wanna *steal* some shit?"

Instant joy lit up his face. "Hell yes!"

Dennison walked into the lunchroom. Her eyes passed over us like a cold wind.

"Here," Tim said. "Sit down, make like we're just eating."

I sat in an open seat across from him. I could see Beef and Ralph staring at me openmouthed from my old table. I looked at them like I'd never seen them before.

"Okay," Tim said. "*Hell yes*, I want to steal some shit."

A couple other kids, Fred and Phillip N., the coolest kid of all, were listening.

"All right," I said. "We're going to steal from the Rite Aid during recess."

"Holy shit!" Tim said. "That's the ultimate. That's the fucking ultimate!"

"Wait," said blond, smooth Phillip N. in a voice that had been cool since birth, a voice that held mysterious essences of middle-school ultra-popularity in suspension. "There's a fence."

"Yeah," I said. "I thought of that."

Actually I hadn't. I tended to ignore physical obstacles. A drawback of my computer-game education.

"I know how we can get through that fence," said Fred.

"How?" Phillip asked.

"Okay," said Fred quickly. "First we need to distract Mrs. Hughes. Then—"

"Jesus," said Tim. "Enough of this fucking talk. I thought we were going to *steal* some shit."

We wolfed down the rest of our lunch and hit the basketball court. Fred's idea was a simple one. At the far end of the court, a corner of the fence had come loose from the pole. He proposed bashing the loose fence with a large rock until it peeled back far enough to permit a single eighth-grade body to wriggle through.

One problem. The lunch monitor, Mrs. Hughes.

Phillip N. eyed her.

"She's small enough," he said.

"It can be done," said Fred.

"What are you talking about?" I asked.

"You came in the middle of last winter, right?" asked Phillip.

I nodded.

"So you're new to this. Well you're about to see some shit. Fred, go get 'em. Tim, you get the rock and get ready to start bashing that fence."

Mrs. Hughes eyed us nervously. Fred ran over to the football field. When he came back around the corner, he was trailed by every eighth-grade boy. Fifteen or sixteen kids altogether. Even Beef was there, in the middle of the pack. He didn't look too happy about it. He was being dragged from the front and pushed from behind, but he was there. Everyone was there. The pack came to a halt at the far end of the court. Fred and a tall kid named Dan gave orders and everyone crowded in tight.

Mrs. Hughes began to walk toward the school building.

"Now!" yelled Fred.

The pack of kids began jogging toward her.

Mrs. Hughes began to run.

She was *way* too slow.

The pack hit her at medium speed and she hit the ground in slow motion. I couldn't believe my eyes.

"Like a bulldozer," Tim marveled.

"Dennison'll do something," Phillip N. said. "But she can't do much. She can't kick out all the boys in the eighth grade. The school would go broke."

These guys are serious, I thought. These Catholic school kids in the boonies are no joke. They're like animals, I thought.

Hughes was up now, brushing dirt off her pants, yelling. The pack of kids dissolved, helpless with laughter. Even Beef was giggling. I turned to the fence. Tim had bashed the corner loose. He stood up, pulling back the links to show a hole Mrs. Hughes could have walked through without ducking her head.

"Damn," I said.

"Dennison will be out here with Mr. Jones and Father O'Connor in two seconds," said Phillip. "But the fence is ready. We'll go tomorrow."

Tim let go of the fence and it sprung back as Dennison and Mr. Jones rounded the corner of the building.

We didn't go tomorrow. The government came down on us hard and fast. Dennison gave every boy in the eighth-grade detention for two weeks. Two weeks of staying after school for an hour and copying out Bible passages. Plus, all our parents grounded us. They were particularly incensed because detention forced us to miss the buses. They had to pick us up personally. I didn't care. I didn't even mind copying the Bible verses. Some of that stuff was crazy.

"*Whoever causes one of these little ones who believe in me to sin, it would be better for him if a great millstone were hung round his neck and he were thrown into the sea.*"

Walk the plank! Even the Bible has pirate wisdom. I copied out the verses with relish. When Dennison wasn't looking I drew pictures of pirate ships in the margins.

Detention wasn't the end, either. All the parents of the guilty boys had to attend a special conference at the school. Dennison really stirred them up. Mom came home from it raging.

"I didn't even do anything," I said as soon as she walked in the door. "I wasn't even part of it."

"But you watched," she said. "You were like the Germans during World War II who just watched the atrocities and didn't help."

The metaphor was uncharacteristically extreme for my mother. Those are Dennison's words, I thought. Plus, World War II had nothing to do with it. We were trying to get *past* World War II. This was piracy. We were trying to move into the future. But Mom wouldn't understand the movement.

"I *did* help," was all I said.

"The kids in that school are rotten to the core," Mom said. "They sound like little Hitlers. Maybe we should put you in the public school."

"No!" I yelled.

Her eyes widened.

"You've been bugging us to go to public school for years."

"I know," I said. "But I think another change would be tough for me. After the *divorce* and all."

That word was enough to banish all talk of school. Mom plunged into bewailing my condition as the child of a single-parent mother, a lowly state she saw existing somewhere on the social scale between wife of a child molester and son of a convict.

But much worse than detention or my mother's painful comparison of me to a Nazi sympathizer was the two-week ban on recess. After we were done eating, we had to sit at our desks and copy out more Bible verses while the girls flounced by us on their way to cavort in the beautiful fall weather.

Me, Phillip N., and Tim were the only ones not involved in the pack that cannonballed Mrs. Hughes. But rather than giving us any special privilege, this fact seemed to blacken us in Dennison's eyes.

"I know what you three are up to," she whispered one afternoon as we filed out after detention.

But any feeling of foreboding was quite canceled by the thrill of having my name conjoined with two social luminaries like Tim and Phillip. I found plenty of ways to capitalize on this association.

"Yeah, it was crazy," I told Allison on the bus one day. "Mrs. Hughes went flying like five feet in the air. I had a real good view, you know, 'cause Phillip N. and Tim and me were talking together when it happened."

"What were you guys talking about?" she asked.

"I can't say."

"Oh, come on," she begged.

"I can't say, but Phillip N. and Tim and me have a plan. We're probably going to talk about it over at Phillip's house after school this week."

"Phillip invited you to his house after school?" Her eyebrows arched.

A little jolt of anxiety went through me. Phillip had issued no such invitation.

"I'm not sure what day we'll be able to do it," I said vaguely. "I'm pretty busy, you know."

But by the time the ban on recess had been lifted, Phillip still hadn't invited me over to his house. Despite that, I was making progress, both social and piratical. Tim, Phillip, and I sat together during detention and lunch, and we'd planned our stealing expedition down to the last detail. I'd even gone to Rite Aid after church one Sunday to scope out the candy aisles. The only item we seriously considered stealing was candy, of course. At thirteen, we were too old to enjoy candy with the same total delight as eleven, but still too young for tobacco or alcohol. Thirteen is an awkward age. At eleven you want candy. At fifteen you want beer. At thirteen you want stolen candy.

For me, of course, the primary value of the stolen candy was as start-up goods to get our pirate economy going. And once that started, who knew what would happen? A black market in stolen candy could grow to gather in baseball cards, sports equipment, computer games—who knew where it would end? Eventually we might even be able to *buy* the fucking school. Don't laugh. In *Pirates!*, I had enough gold to buy a whole city. At a minimum, our pirate economy would utterly undermine Dennison and her whole regime. I broke it down for Phillip at lunch. He was talking about getting all the kids to yell out "fuck" in the middle of science class.

"That's no good," I said. "Whatever we do, Dennison wins."

"What do you mean?" he asked.

"I mean, all we're doing is breaking her rules. We don't do anything on our own. She's got a rule, and we try to break it."

"Yeah," he said. "So what? Breaking rules is fun. Everyone yelling out 'fuck' in class at the same time? That's fun, man."

I waved the banana I was eating.

"Dennison could make a rule that you can't have bananas for lunch," I said. "And then this banana right here would suddenly become fun. Eating it would suddenly become funny."

"And your point is?"

"*She's* the one who decides what fun is," I said. "*She's* the one in control."

"That's 'cause she *is* in control," said Phillip. "She's the principal. We're eighth-graders. Duh."

He's a prisoner of common sense, I thought. I tried again.

"We could be doing something in here that she can't control," I said. "We could be doing something on our own. Something really fun. We could turn this whole school inside out."

"Oh yeah, how?" he demanded.

I told him about my idea that we'd sell the stolen candy to other kids. We'd turn recess into a black market. And the market would spread.

"Making money, huh," he said.

His brow furrowed.

"That could be cool," he said. "But don't tell Tim and Fred about it yet. They wouldn't understand. They're just excited about the stealing right now. We'll get them into the plan later."

My heart expanded in my chest. He understood!

"I won't tell anyone," I said. "I only told you 'cause I knew you'd get it."

"Hey," he said. "Fred's coming over after school next Tuesday. You wanna come too?"

It was actually happening.

"You want me to come over to your house after school?" I asked carefully.

He laughed.

"Yeah, man," he said.

I sailed through the rest of the day on clouds. That night when I played *Pirates!*, I pretended Phillip and I were co-captains. We stole sugar from Spanish merchant ships, sold it to black-market Dutchmen. Bought guns. Blew holes in war galleons. Towed the hulks into Trinidad to sell for timber. Bought rum.

The pixilated sun shone on clear blue sea. Shone always. Have I mentioned that there was no nighttime in *Pirates!*? It came out a few years before computer games started adding day-night cycles. Designers thought that having nighttime would give the game worlds more realism. And if *Pirates!* had been designed a few years later, no doubt it would have had nighttime too. That's common sense.

But I prefer to think that it wouldn't. I prefer to think that when all the other games went day-night, *Pirates!* would keep its endless sunshine.

Let me explain. My earliest political memory was of Ronald Reagan proclaiming "Morning in America" on TV when I was eight. I remember asking my dad when it would be "Nighttime in America" and I remember him laughing and saying, It's coming, just you wait, what goes up must come down, night's coming, after the morning comes the night!

But now I knew a place where you could wait for night forever. I believe that the endless sunshine in *Pirates!* wasn't simply due to the fact computer-game night hadn't yet been invented. The endless sunshine was on purpose. It meant something. Something true.

•

The candy heist went off without a hitch. We did it the day the recess ban ended. I played lookout. Superfluous, really. Mrs. Hughes was shell-shocked. She didn't move five steps from the door to the school. If someone approached her, she'd run through the door. No problem. I gave Tim and Fred the signal. Phillip bent back the broken fence. They rushed through the hole with empty backpacks, rushed back eight minutes later with backpacks full.

"Check it out," said Fred, flashing a grin.

He unzipped his backpack and held it out. Snickers and Skittles shone in the October sunlight.

"We'll divide it up at my house tomorrow," said Phillip.

"To sell," I whispered.

He nodded.

That night I had a dream about a pirate ship. The deck was covered with linoleum, just like the floor of a school classroom. Open sky above. Cannons lined the sides. Me and Phillip counted gold. Tim aimed a spyglass at a dark shape on the horizon. I woke in a pool of milky light. The window showed a misty sky, a colorless meadow, and two bored horses. Goodbye dry land, I thought. Time to board ship.

The school day passed slowly amid muffled gestures of forlorn anarchy. Dan passed a note to Tim that said "Fuck." Tim looked furtively around, made sure Mr. Filleto's back was turned before he opened it. He actually put his hand over his mouth to stifle the giggle. Like a girl. Wow, I thought. Dennison's really getting to them.

Hold on, Tim, I thought. The fire is almost out. The last wisps of anarchic smoke are disappearing, but hold on. To-morrow we're going to put anarchy on numbers.

But first I had to get to Phillip's house so we could price the candy and fill everyone in on the plan. And there was a problem. The driver of the bus that Phillip took home wouldn't let a new kid on without a note from the school.

"And it's gotta be signed by Dennison," hissed the driver. "None of your tricks. I know you kids and your tricks."

The man couldn't be reasoned with, lied to, or tricked. I ended up on my usual bus, gritting my teeth through the twist-ing, painfully slow, hour-long ride to my house. Mine was the very last stop, of course. Talk about the boonies. After Met-tawa the map's blank.

It seemed I'd never get to Phillip's. At home I writhed in furious impatience while Mom called Mrs. N. to get the direc-tions and then chatted for ten full minutes, languidly drawing curlicues around the street names as she listened.

"Oh, I think these kids have learned their lesson," Mom said into the phone, looking at me.

By the time we finally pulled up to Phillip's house, it was almost five. And as impatient as I'd been for the past two hours, the funny thing was that as soon as Mom drove off, I discovered I was in no hurry to go in.

I must have lingered before Phillip's door for five minutes. This is it, I thought. I took a deep breath. Six weeks ago I was sitting next to Beef and now here I am, looking at Phillip N.'s door. The gateway to middle-school royalty. The only royalty, really. You never care about status the way you do in eighth grade. Here I am before the door to Phillip N.'s house, I thought, and in one second I'm going to knock and it's going to open and I'm going to pass through it.

I knocked. When his mom opened the door, the odor of

the house, a subtle fragrance of an absolutely cool substance heated to room temperature, leaked into the October air like water into oil.

"Oh, you must be Michael C.," she said. "Well, I'm Phillip N.'s mother!"

She beamed at me. I looked down at my feet.

"Oh, Phillip," she called into the house. "Your *friend* is here!"

I looked up, my fear banished by that magic syllable. I imagined Allison pointing at me, turning to one of her pretty friends and saying, "That's him. *A friend of Phillip N.'s.*" Phillip and I were friends. And I—we—were about to become something else. Pirates! My spine uncurled and the pent-up energy of six weeks flooded my limbs. Okay, I thought. I'm back. The prestige of Phillip's house had cowed me for a minute, but now I was back on my game.

Phillip came out of the gloom wiping something from his mouth. Adrenaline vibrated in my legs.

"Oh, hey, man," he said. "Cool."

"Let's get down to business!" I said.

He smiled.

"Let's go on down, man. The guys are in my room."

I followed him down carpeted stairs into the finished basement.

"I think we should price the Snickers at a quarter," I said. "The big ones, I mean. Everyone can afford that. And anyway, the point isn't to make money at first, it's just to get things going, so it's important to have a price that everyone—"

"Yeah, man," said Phillip. "Like, I mean, whatever."

He opened the door to his room and my new life ended.

Tim and Fred and Dan sat cross-legged on the floor. Bags of candy were strewn across the carpet, but I hardly noticed that. What drew my gaze like a magnet were the faces.

The faces. Three faces slit with crescent-shaped holes. You could see the chocolate through the holes. Jaws working. They never stopped. Two and a half Snickers bars disappeared while I stared. A smell like chocolate mixed with hot human insides poured from the face holes. And the talking bubbled out of those brown smiles as they chewed, the talking never stopped.

"Man, fuck Dennison, she—"

"Oh totally, she can't even fuck with us, we can do whatever the fuck we want matter of fact we can—"

"Man, do you remember when that chair hit the damn blades? Do you remember? Do you?"

"Do you remember the look on Beef's face? When Dan made that fake fart?"

"Pass those Skittles."

"They're gone."

"You pig!"

"You're a pig."

"Hey, Clune," said Tim. "What's up? Want a Snickers?"

He looked at me with sugar-drunk eyes. He looked at me with eyes full of drowned futures. He looked at me with eyes the color of the sea at night.

"No I don't want a fucking Snickers," I said.

The smiles froze.

"Hey, what's your problem, man?" asked Fred.

I'm not going to cry, I told myself. I dug my nails into my palms.

I forced a smile into my face. Like forcing a fist down the mouth of a beer bottle.

"Nothing's wrong," I said through my teeth. "Gimme a Snickers."

The smiles lengthened again. The jaws started working. And that's how it was everywhere. That's how it was all over the world. That's how it was everywhere as 1988 turned into 1989 and Communism vanished and for a brief moment Capitalism stood alone.

For a brief moment Capitalism finally stood all alone as 1988 turned into 1989, and when there are two things each must be itself, but when there is only one thing it can be anything. Capitalism could be anything. What would it be? A pirate ship or an office building? Anticipation lit up the world from the Kremlin to St. Joe's.

The world trembled and watched for the first skull and crossbones to go up on the roof of a bank, a school, a post office, a car dealership, a church. And all over the world as 1988 turned into 1989 the pirates ate their candy. They smiled and talked and ate their candy, and it was only candy after all. And they weren't pirates after all, they were only children.

And when the candy was gone, it was time to grow up. When we were done eating our candy, it was time to grow up and to move from the office buildings of school into the office buildings of work. It was time to move from the office buildings of the past into the office buildings of the future.

7.

A Heart of Sky

That spring my new friends disappeared. Their faces just closed up. I couldn't understand it. One day people stopped talking to me. Maybe it was the piracy scheme. Maybe it was my cheap shoes. I should have asked before it was too late. I should have asked someone what I'd done, how I'd fucked up. There might have been a moment, walking out to recess with Phillip maybe, when I could have asked him.

Everything cool with us?

And he would have frowned, shaken his head, thought for a second, told me. And I would have apologized, then promised, then pleaded. It might have worked. Sometime in the past couple of weeks, I thought, there had been a moment when the faces were closing and I could've slipped in an apology, a promise, something.

There's always that moment. I know that now. That's why now, when I speak to the people close to me, I watch their faces carefully. Even when we're both laughing, I watch their faces carefully. A face can close in the middle of laughter. I've seen it.

If you watch carefully, you can spot a closing face. And if you spot it, you have a chance. But that first time in eighth grade, I missed it. By the time I noticed what was happening, it had happened. It was too late. When everyone's not talking to you there's no one to ask.

It was like I'd gone deaf. In the halls between classes I moved in a loose bag of silence. The kids stood whispering in knots, and when I walked past, their faces lost expression. Fred, Phillip, Tim, Allison, Carl, even Beef. They looked at me like they were posing for photographs.

Not family photographs. Art photographs. Like the ones I'd seen at the art museum during the school field trip in sixth grade. I lingered by those glass-framed photos while the rest of class walked ahead, following the dutiful drone of the guide. Those were the first color photos I'd ever seen where the subjects didn't smile. The photographer who takes these pictures doesn't say "cheese," I thought. I wondered what he did say.

Pretend you're one thousand years old.

Pretend you've been looking at the sky for a whole hour.

Pretend you are the desert.

Every kid's face I saw during the May of my last year of middle school looked like that. Like art. Art makes you see things in a new way. I saw faces in a new way. The way faces look when they're not *for* you, when they haven't got anything *for* you.

I sat in class in silence. I walked in silence down the halls. At the top of the torsos, the kids' faces swiveled around. After a week, they all started to look the same. Their personalities burned up in their faces, like a picture burning in a frying pan. The hallway between classes: a line of torsos, topped by flesh-colored frying pans.

After the second week of silence the faces stopped looking the same. Strange differences became visible. Important differences. I even began to wonder how anyone could ever call these things by the same word. "Faces." The twin liquid pools near the top, sure, each face had that. The eyes. But those were the least interesting part of the faces now. The least face-like. When a face isn't *for* you, the eyes lose their witchcraft and you realize that in fact the face has very little to do with the eyes.

They say the soul is in the eyes, but the face is in the cheeks. That's what I learned during the last month of middle school. By the end of the month, when I saw a face, my gaze slid right to the cheeks. The eyes were nothing, identical drops of water. Nothing. The cheeks . . . Handsbreadths of sand, no two the same color. Some freckled, some lit in spots by early pimples. In some the cheekbones swelled under the flesh like a shark moving in shallow water. In some the cheekbones pushed out like tiny reverse footprints. In others you couldn't see bone at all.

Just three weeks ago, I thought, just a few weeks ago, if someone had asked me what I thought about cheeks I would have said they were crazy. Cheeks? A cheek is a cheek, I would have said. Empty flesh. A covering for the bones that support the eyes and mouth. And now . . .

"Hey."

The cheek moved, jolting me from my reflections. I recognized Allison's voice, close. It was after English class. Thursday of the third week of silence.

"Oh, hi, Allison."

I looked at her cheek.

"Here," she said.

Her cheek flushed. Like sunrise in the desert. Beautiful, I thought. I blinked rapidly, looked down at the card she thrust toward me. Looked up, but it was like looking through the wrong end of a telescope. I couldn't get her face in the right focus for talking.

"I . . . uh . . ."

She was gone. I looked down at the card. Print-shop palm trees framed five lines of text.

Hey Grads!
POOL PARTY
To Celebrate
THE END OF MIDDLE SCHOOL

The last line held an address I assumed was Allison's, and a date. Saturday. *Allison*, I thought, clutching the card. I read the words over and over, as if they contained a secret code. Maybe this is a message! I thought. Excitement tightened my chest. Allison invited me to her party! Allison still likes me! She's afraid to talk to me in school in front of the others, but at her house, it'll be different.

When I got home that afternoon, I proudly showed my mom the card.

"Allison's the most popular girl in school," I said.

Then, gingerly, I asked Mom if she could drive me. A delicate subject.

"Of course I can!"

Her unexpected eagerness took me aback. Mom was never eager to drive anywhere. In fact she'd do almost anything to avoid having to drive me. Jenny and I were the only kids who lived this far from school who took the bus. The other kids who lived near us, their moms drove them. We alone rode the bus. At first the school refused to send the bus out this far. They had a policy. It had taken Mom almost a week to get the policy changed.

"It's prejudice," she'd yelled into the phone.

She waited, drumming her fingers on the counter while the school official on the other end tried to explain.

"So my children can't have what everyone else has because of where they live? That's prejudice."

Jenny and I looked out the huge kitchen windows at the nearest mansion, looming across five acres of our land. Prejudice, I thought.

"We don't have a car," Mom lied.

Jenny rolled her eyes. Mom was just getting started. When dealing with officials, she had no problem saying the most humiliating things. She used self-humiliation like currency.

"We don't have a car."

"I'm too depressed to drive."

"My medication makes me dangerous behind the wheel."

On one of the early calls she somehow found out that the short bus didn't have the same distance limit as the regular bus. That night at dinner I caught her looking at Jenny in a new way.

"You're not very good at math, Jenny," she said.

"I guess not," Jenny said.

"Yeah, but are you *really* bad at math? What's thirty divided by five?"

"Six," Jenny said.

"No, it's seven," said Mom.

"Are you retarded, Mom?" I blurted out. "Thirty divided by five is six."

"No, I'm not retarded," Mom said in a quiet voice. "But your sister may be."

When it came to avoiding driving us through the vast spaces that separated every point from every other in the distant suburbs she'd moved us to, Mom was serious. And yet now she was inexplicably eager to drive me to Allison's party.

"You'll drive me?" I asked dubiously.

"Of course I will!" she said. "It'll be good for you. You haven't gone over to a friend's house in weeks."

I looked down.

"What's going on with you, anyway?" Mom asked.

I didn't say anything.

"What happened to that boy Fred?" she asked. "You were over at his house two, three times a week this winter. And what about your friend Phillip? Or that other one, Tim? Aren't you guys friends anymore?"

I looked at my shoes.

"I don't know," I said.

Mom put her hands to her face.

"*They've stopped talking to you*," she gasped.

It wasn't a question.

"What did you *do*, Michael?"

"I don't know," I said. "Nothing, I don't know, I just . . ."

She grabbed my hands.

"*Think*," she said. "It can be the littlest thing. Something you'd never think twice about. Trust me, I know. Maybe it's not too late! *Think*. Why did they stop talking to you? When did it happen?"

I didn't know what to say. I just stood there with my hands in hers, staring at her red, heaving cheek.

•

Saturday was sunny, all blue and gold. It was still early enough in the season that good weather hadn't lost the power to dazzle, almost to kill.

"I'm going home for a nap after I drop you off," Mom said. "This sun just takes it out of me."

She glared at me in the rearview mirror.

"Now I want you to have a *good time* at this party, Michael," she said. "This could be your *last chance*. Trust me. I know how it is with people."

The Suburban drove past twigs, signs, brown grass, and puddles, all stricken by the total blue sky. Everything was stricken, holding up its late-spring color ineffectually against the pouring blue power. The galaxy burned and melted in the blue fire of the sky.

A man stood by the side of the road in a yellow and brown hot dog suit, advertising a new takeout place. The light pouring from the sky faded the brown of the hot dog suit to white, faded the mustard yellow to white, faded the man's flesh to nothing. To air.

At the party the kids stood in sun-whitened swimsuits and colorless bodies. I looked hopefully at their cheeks. Allison stood next to her mother near the diving board.

"Hello!" said the mother. "You must be, um."

She turned to Allison, but Allison just stared at me silently. I looked in vain for my reflection in her sun-canceled eyes. I walked away.

Phillip and Fred laughed in the corner of the yard, but when I walked up to them their faces lost expression. I thought, Their cheeks are nearly see-through in this sun. I sat at the edge of the pool, kicking my legs in the water.

Allison's parents' faces were full of worried eyes. I could hear their thoughts. *Who's that one sitting alone by the edge of the pool? Who's that one the others won't look at?*

When they turned their eyes from me, I snuck inside and called home.

"Hello?"

Mom's sleepy voice.

"I, uh. Mom? I think I'm ready to come home now."

"You've only been there, what? Half an hour? I just got back."

"I think I'm ready to come home now."

"They're not talking to you."

Her voice suddenly sleepless. Allison's mother had crept into the room, watching me.

"I'll wait for you outside," I said into the phone.

"Are they listening?" said Mom. "Do the parents know?"

I hung up. Allison's mom stepped closer. Coils of blue sky sparked in her platinum blond hair. I stood in my dry swimsuit facing her.

"Is everything okay? Um . . ."

"Michael," I said. "My name is Michael. I have to go now."

•

When we got home, I did what I'd done every afternoon since my friends stopped talking to me. I played *Might and Magic II*. I plopped down in my computer chair with relief, longing to escape the tension, the deepening silence of the kids like a constantly hissing gas.

And at first, in the beginning, the game did seem like an escape. Superficially, it resembled *The Bard's Tale II* in its *D&D*–derived gameplay and fantasy world. The story line was familiar. The good king had been overthrown and you were supposed to help him reclaim his rightful place and save the world from an evil wizard.

But the generic plot contained unsettling, discordant elements. For example, the fantasy world, full of the usual unicorns, goblins, and demons, had the unusual name CRON, which stood for Central Research Observational Nacelle. This was the first hint that *Might and Magic II* was something new. CRON. What a name for a fantasy world. Central Research Observational Nacelle. Was I the researcher or the researched? The observed or the observer? And what was a Nacelle? I imagined scientists staring coldly out at me through their unicorn or demon costumes.

The second hint lay in its graphic design. At first glance, the screen looked like another *Bard's Tale* knock-off. The bottom half of the display listed your party members, their hit points, and their armor class. The top right quarter showed either a list of the party's enemies, if you were in battle, or a map of the area, if you were in a dungeon or castle.

The top left quarter of the screen, however, was genuinely new. It showed a 3-D view of the world. I'd played other games that had represented vaguely three-dimensional dungeons with lines and parallelograms. *Ultima IV*, for instance. Even *The Bard's Tale II* had attempted something similar. But *Might and Magic II*, with its sophisticated modeling of perspective and shading effects, was the first game I'd ever played with an identifiably realistic element. It was the first game that incorporated an element of reality. Like an imaginary angel or demon holding out a real hand. I didn't know if I wanted to grasp it.

I examined the graphics carefully. They looked pretty realistic, but . . . There was a subtle warp in the game's realism. Something's wrong with this 3-D, I thought. I stared at the screen. This 3-D, it has something, something . . . *effervescent*. That's the only word I could think of. I'd heard the word on a commercial for a new soda. *Effervescent*, the woman's voice had whispered over the image of rising diamond bubbles. And now I stared at the screen showing a fantasy medieval town's main street, and I thought: *This is effervescent.*

I couldn't put my finger on it. The street dwindled into the distance before me. The paving was stone. Nothing effervescent about stone. Nothing effervescent about perspective. On either side of the street, low walls rose. Walls are not effervescent. But . . . weirdly low walls . . . Why were the walls so low?

Low walls. And then I saw it. The secret of *Might and Magic's* 3-D, the secret that seduced me into playing in three dimensions: low walls. The walls of the dungeon or town or castle only came halfway up the display. You could always see the tops of the walls. And above them, the sky. Anywhere you went in CRON, you could always see the sky, settling on the tops of the walls and buildings and trees and mountains. Resting on them. Rising behind them. The sky *molded* the shapes of the world. The sky was the third dimension.

The basic sensation of 3-D is the sensation that an object has a behind, a reverse, a back side. In *Might and Magic II*, the sky established this back side. The sky, folded behind the leering goblin. The sky, expanding on the far side of the tower. What's behind the *Might and Magic* image? The sky, always the sky. The constant presence of the infinite sky gave the walls and towers of this imaginary world their definition, their realistic shape.

And here is the paradox. The sky, as everyone knows, is the least realistic element of the real world. It just looks unreal. The Vikings believed it to be the blue skull of a giant. Medieval Christians saw it as the veil of heaven. It has always been easy for humans to believe the most fantastical things about the sky. To look up at the sky in the middle of a busy street is to be somewhere else. It's already to be playing a kind of game. So it made sense that when computer games began to tire of living outside reality, when computer games began to dream of *including* reality, they began by imitating the sky.

And they succeeded. The sky turned out to be easy for even the relatively primitive graphics of late-eighties computer games to represent. *Might and Magic II*'s success at creating believable skies showed something about the potential of computing graphics, true, but also, and more important, it showed something about the sky.

Might and Magic discovered that the sky could be used to make the walls and trees of its fantasy world look more real. But ask yourself. Doesn't this discovery tell us something about *our* world? The next time you see a person or town or tower against the blue sky, the next time the sky supplies the third dimension of the image before you, ask yourself: Does this look real or unreal? If the sky is the principle of reality in the computer game, isn't it also the principle of unreality in our world?

There is a point where technology and nature switch places.

•

We—my party of two knights, a ninja, an archer, and two wizards—began the game in the town of Middlegate. The ninja's name was Allison. The knights were Fred and Phillip. Our first job, as in all computer role-playing games, was to accumulate enough experience, weaponry, and armor to be able to defend ourselves against the fearsome beasts that waited outside the town walls. I studied the map of CRON that came with the game, formulated a plan. When the party was ready, we'd take the high road to the Luxus Palace Royale. The bartender in Middlegate whispered that the king was last seen there. That's where we'd search for clues to the king's disappearance.

So we sharpened our skills on the hordes of thieves and goblins that hid in the dark alleys of Middlegate. Time passed. *Might and Magic II* had time. The sky told the time. After several hours the bright blue sky and white clouds would dissolve, revealing starfields. Then outer space itself supplied the towers and walls with their third dimension.

We hunted thieves. A band of twenty thieves burst under our swords and arrows in a rich dust of numbers. And when the dust cleared, the upper left corner of the screen showed a treasure chest. Outer space behind and above it. A real 3-D chest, holding imaginary gold. We took the gold and bought supplies from Edmund's Expeditions, a small shop on the far side of the town, near the gates, under the sky.

Eventually, feeling strong enough, we ventured outside the town, into the roads and fields of CRON. A troop of purple-scaled, sky-spangled dragons promptly reduced us to ash.

I looked at the blue sky above the corpses of my party. Un-blinking, staring at it as long as I could. I filled myself with that sky. Then I shut my burning eyes, got up from my chair, felt my way along the wall.

"What are you doing, Michael?" Sean asked from the couch where he was watching cartoons.

"Nothing," I said.

I hit my toe against a chair, gritted my teeth.

"Are your eyes gone away, Michael?" Sean asked.

"Gone away," I said.

He clapped. My fingers touched the cold glass of the great room's sliding door. The blue sky of CRON was fading behind my eyes, like the slow fade of color and shapes when I turned off the monitor. I had to hurry.

My fingers scraped along the glass until I felt the handle. I pressed in the release, slid the door over the rusting tracks. Cool spring air on my face. I stepped out, the pebbles of the patio sharp on my bare feet. The warmth of the sun on my lifted face. I opened my eyes.

And it was as if the monitor had been turned back on.

"Your eyes are back, Michael," said Sean. He stood beside me, squinting up at the blue sky, the blinding white clouds.

"Yes," I said.

"What are you doing?" he asked.

"I think," I said, "I think I've made a discovery."

"What's a discovery?" Sean asked.

He'd dragged Stinky after him onto the patio. He looked up at me, wonder dilating his small face. I was going to tell him to go back inside, but then I stopped. This is my little brother, I thought.

"Sean," I said, "do you remember when you woke up Mom and told her that Jesus was in your room?"

He nodded.

"And what did she tell you?"

"She told me it was a dream," Sean said. "She told me Jesus wasn't in my room."

"And where did she tell you Jesus was?"

Sean pointed to his head. I nodded.

"Okay," I said. "Jesus was imaginary. He wasn't really in your room. He was in your dream, in your head. Well, you know that game I'm playing on the computer?"

Sean nodded.

"Okay," I said. "Well, I had a feeling that there's something in the game that's exactly the same as something out here in the world. That's why I closed my eyes and came out here. To see if it's *exactly* the same. And you know what? It is!"

Sean looked up at me, puzzled. I sighed.

"It's kind of like I've found a way to see Jesus for real," I told him. "Out here in the world."

Sean's face lit up.

"Where?" he asked breathlessly.

I pointed at the sky. Sean nodded.

"Oh yes," he said solemnly. "That's where Jesus is."

•

At school they were taking pictures for the yearbook. They called us in fives, alphabetically. When the nun called my name, I trooped out with Ralph, Beef, Phillip's girlfriend, Danielle, and a girl named Mary. The guys and girls began whispering to each other. I stood in the middle, listening. It wasn't often these days that I got to stand close enough to other kids to hear what they said.

"He got it from Tim," Danielle whispered.

"Well, where'd Tim get it?" asked Mary.

"From his older brother."

"Well, has Phillip tried it?"

Danielle nodded.

"Well, have you tried it?"

"*Gross*," Danielle hissed. "God, who do you think I *am*, Mary?"

The girls dissolved in giggles.

I turned my head toward the boys.

"You're sick, Beef," Ralph was muttering.

"No, I'm just saying," said Beef.

"And I'm saying you're sick."

"I can get it from my uncle," said Beef.

"My dad says your uncle is white trash," said Ralph.

"No, I'm just saying I can get it from my uncle," said Beef.

Ralph was silent.

"We could, like, hang out with Fred and Phillip if we did it," said Beef.

"You ever hear of peer pressure?" asked Ralph.

"Yeah, it's what your *mom* does," said Beef.

He laughed.

"You're retarded," said Ralph.

The door to the office opened.

"Ralph Anscombe!" an unfamiliar male voice called out.

Ralph walked through the door.

"Peer pressure is what his *mom* does," Beef said, turning to me.

For a split second we stood face-to-face, his goofy grin frozen on his lips. Then his grin went out of focus, lost definition. He turned away.

"What were you talking about, Beef?" I whispered. "What does your uncle have?"

The girls suddenly stopped giggling.

"Don't tell him," said Danielle in an icy voice.

"I'm not saying anything!" Beef said.

He couldn't look at Danielle without looking at me too. So he stood with his face motionless on his neck, staring at the wall across the hallway.

"I'll tell Phillip," said Danielle.

"Come on," Beef whined, staring at the wall. "I didn't say anything."

"Kurt Bolowski," the male voice intoned.

Ralph walked out of the room. Beef walked in. The girls turned away from me, whispered so low I couldn't hear them.

"Michael Clune," the voice boomed.

I walked in. An old man with cheeks like a frozen waterfall pointed at a stool. A felt backdrop of sky blue hung behind the stool. I climbed onto it, turned toward the blinding lights.

"Say cheese," the man said.

•

I'm invisible, I thought.

Adrenaline thrilled in my throat. Two hours after the photo session, recess. Clear blue sky above. I walked right through a knot of boys playing dominoes. Tim and Nick expertly stepped out of my way without looking at me. The conversation didn't flag. I stood for three whole seconds in the middle of their game. They threw the dice between my legs. They leaned around me to taunt the loser and cheer the winner.

I'm totally invisible, I thought. Not totally, I thought. It wouldn't work with adults. Not yet, anyway. But if there were enough kids around I could just disappear.

•

I'd been venturing out farther into CRON. There were still lots of things that could kill my party in seconds, but there were also a few we could kill. The giant beetles, for instance. And the jugglers. And even a Windmare, if it appeared alone.

Every day I inched a few paces farther up the path the map showed leading to the Luxus Palace Royale. Then, the day the image of my face was captured against a field of sky blue, we made it. For the first time, we saw the palace in the distance. Within reach. Five, six moves away. The Luxus Palace! A chord of white towers, struck against the blue sky. A brace of dragons stalked us, but we'd bought potions that gave us the speed of Windmares, and we flew up the broad yellow pavement with dragon flame licking our heels.

Inside the palace, black tile shone. The walls were sky blue. We opened a portal. A tall black bishop killed us in a room shaped like a star.

The next day, at recess, I went back to the knot of kids playing dominoes, and sat invisible, looking up at the sky. The dice clattered around me, and the voices . . . After a while the sounds of the kids were almost natural. Like flowing water, bird chirps. *More* than natural. Being in the midst of people who won't talk to you, who won't know you, surrounded by faces that aren't *for* you, by words whizzing *over* and *around* you—it's like being alone with nature. It's like being alone with nature, only more so.

I looked up at the sky, and then I remembered something. Something about the sky. Something important. I remembered driving with my father, I must have been six or seven. He was running errands. Winter. Dirty white snow lined the roads. A song came on the radio, an Irish folk song, "The Fields of

Athenry." My father parked the car, leaped out to run into a store. He left the car running, heat pouring through the vents. I wriggled out of my jacket. Looked through the cold glass of the window, at a sky of soft blue.

The blue didn't seem to belong to the winter afternoon. An hour before, the sky had been steel white; an hour later it would be steel gray. Now this sky of soft blue, slipped between metal slats. Fuzzy blue, as if the color was blurred by the distance it had traveled. The distance it was traveling.

Blue. The color of passing time. Soft blue. A color that could have been anywhere, that didn't belong to the winter afternoon. And the Irish folk song kept playing:

Low lie the fields of Athenry
Where once we watched the small free birds fly

And I thought: I will stay like this forever.

Looking through the car window at the blue sky. What was blue color outside was a quiet feeling inside me and I thought: I will stay like this forever. Peace, I thought. Like they say in church. *Peace.* I don't care that I have to go on these errands with Dad instead of playing with Eric. Peace. I don't care that I have to be in this car for all these errands. Peace. I can stay here forever. Nothing can harm me (peace), nothing can bother me. There's something inside me that won't change. The unchanging thing inside me has a color. The color is sky blue. I looked out the windows at it.

And when my father got back in the car the feeling lasted, this feeling of a feeling that lasts. It was the feeling that the sky-blue feeling would last forever. That was the feeling I had looking at the sky. Strange, a feeling curled around on itself, like the Aztecs represent the sky as a blue snake eating its tail.

I had a feeling like that. It wasn't a feeling you have in time. It was the feeling of time stretching out forever inside the feeling it was. That was the feeling. Its color was sky blue.

The song ended, the feeling lasted. It lasted through the next errand, and the next. It lasted as Dad turned the big car toward home. The feeling lasted as we entered our block, and then it skipped six or seven years.

Sitting invisible inside the knot of kids at recess, with their voices blurred and smudged and *blued* by social distance, I looked up at the blue sky, remembered sitting in my father's car with "The Fields of Athenry" and the blue sky, and then I wasn't remembering. It was back.

•

There was a time machine in CRON, too. After six tries, the black bishop lay dead, splayed out in the center of the star-shaped room, our spells sparking in his ebony eyes. Behind him lay a door, and behind the door stood a courtier. The courtier told us of the time machine. His words unfurled on the right side of the screen while his lithe, purple-clad body twirled above black tile on the left.

A time machine, I thought. The king is lost not in space but in time, I thought. But the time machine is hidden in space, I thought. A snake eating its tail . . .

"Where is the time machine?" I asked the courtier.

"Follow the message," he said. "The message in the garden."

We retraced our steps, passing the dead body of the bishop, fighting through a horde of angry jugglers, evading a surprisingly deadly unicorn. To the throne room.

"Find the message," whispered the queen across the right hand of the screen. "The message in the garden."

We fled down corridors, searching for the garden.

"Seek the answer in the garden," said the dwarf.

"Find the message in the garden," read the scroll in the treasure chest.

We raced through the palace, doubling back through mazes of corridors, then doubling back again. Until finally, pushing open a nondescript wooden door I was sure we'd already searched, trying it out of sheer desperation, pushing it open and then:

Blue sky over low garden walls.

Giant flowers whirring softly at the top of thick stems.

A stone pedestal, covered with writing.

We crept closer. The letters and words and sentences of the message came into focus:

F e iuteeustj ceetuF i virs ri sAb aaoritrs
o a ivaoc eehu whss na eTeno aoacs bciltsth k
r c nil ot,eer h i Mtr wrl uopptl. Readlh het.
 h dd bmr y irdao v .a gpfprea orn ew ia

I slumped back in my chair. What did it mean? A scrambled message, a code. I grabbed the game box, checked the back. "For ages 12 and up." I was thirteen. Okay, I thought. I can solve this.

I went upstairs and got a pencil and a piece of paper. Got to work. Rearranging the letters of the first few words was hopeless. The first word was a single letter: "F." Nothing I could do with that.

Then inspiration struck. Instead of reading across the rows of letters, I tried reading *down* them. F-O-R. A word! Keep going. E-A-C-H. Another! Two words: "For Each." I was on my way.

But reading down the next row, I saw two I's together.

That didn't look good. I couldn't think of any words that had two I's together. With a sinking feeling I spelled it out, anyway.

"For each iind."

That just didn't make sense. Or did it? Was "iind" an acronym? I already knew the game used acronyms. CRON, for example. Yes, it had to be. Reading down had produced two clear words. "IIND" was clearly part of the message. An acronym. Okay. What could I stand for?

Interstellar.
Inside
Internal
Interior
I (meaning me)

I picked up the pencil and wrote a list of all the words I could think of beginning with I. Then I did the same for N and D. Method, that was the key. Method could solve anything. By the time the room had darkened and the smell of Mom preparing dinner began to float in, I had my three lists, one for each letter. I began methodically to combine them.

For Each Interstellar Interior Nacelle Drive.
For Each I Inside Night Deliver.
For Each Internal I No Doubt.
For Each Icy I No Deliverance.

•

The next day was the second to last Thursday of middle school. I was in the bathroom during math class, in a stall, working on the code. I'd been doing that for the past two days, asking to go to the bathroom in the middle of class and then sitting in the stall working on my code for half an hour, forty minutes, even a whole period once. The teachers didn't seem to care. Maybe they too were losing the ability to see me.

I'd just thought of a new word for D, "Discovery." This word seemed especially promising. This could be the one, I thought.

"For Each I Inside Night, Discover!"

I rubbed my hands with excitement, then froze. The door to the bathroom swung open. I quickly drew my legs up to the toilet seat, stifled my breath. Listened. There were two of them. I recognized their voices at once. Fred and Nick.

"C'mon, hurry," Nick whispered.

"Shut the fuck up, dude," said Fred.

I looked carefully under the stall. I could see their feet, close together. They were standing next to the sinks.

"What if someone comes in?" asked Nick nervously.

"Shove it down your pants."

"They'll see it!"

"Then shove it up your ass."

"That's not funny, Fred. School's almost out. Think I want to get held back over this?"

"Yeah," said Fred. "All I know is that if you *do* get busted, you better keep your fucking mouth shut. You've always been a pussy. If Dennison finds out about this, we'll know exactly whose ass to beat."

"No you won't," Nick replied. "If Dennison finds out, it could be anyone. The whole school knows!"

"They just know the words," said Fred. "*Seven in the morning.* They hear us say the words and they know it means something maybe, but they don't know what it means."

"They know *something*," said Nick. "Mary said she even heard Beef talking about it."

"Just shut the fuck up."

There was a rustling sound. Silence. Then Nick began coughing and spitting, loudly, into the sink.

"Yeah," said Fred. "Hell, yeah."

Sound of running water.

"You cool now?"

"Yeah," said Nick.

His voice sounded shaky. Thirty seconds later, they left.

I cautiously put my feet to the floor. Carefully opened the stall. The sinks were clean. So were the floors. I went to the garbage can, frantically rifled through it. Used Kleenex, candy wrappers, gum, an illicit soda can. What were they doing? What were they hiding?

I looked into the mirror. Tears blurred my vision, blurred my face out. The whole school was in on this thing except me. Some scheme, some plan. Something awesome, that was clear. The total middle-school-ending victory Phillip and Fred and I used to talk about, they'd found it. They had a plan. And I was the only one not in on it.

Seven in the morning. What the hell did that mean? For a second, hope flared—an acronym!—lists unfurled through my mind, method, discovery, victory! Vanished in a second. Fred and Phillip weren't using acronyms. *Seven in the morning.* It could stand for literally anything. You'd have to untwist the knots of Fred's brain to unlock that phrase.

Why had they turned on me? I saw my *Pirates!* scheme in a new light. My plans, they interfered with some deep, secret shit Phillip and Fred had been cooking up. Maybe they'd been cooking it up for years. Maybe they'd only become friends with me to find out my plan, to check it out, to neutralize it. And then they dropped me forever. They'd probably *never* liked me, no one here had *ever* liked me. I'd been fooling myself.

What were they doing? If I could just find out, I could join in. I could be a part of it. I was smart. I could help them not get caught. I could *help* them . . .

I looked down at the crumpled piece of paper in my hand. Unfolded it.

"For Each I Inside Night, Discover."

I hurled it into the toilet.

•

My emotions cooled on the long bus ride home. When I got inside, I felt a little better. Calmer. Ate a granola bar, played soccer out back with Sean for a while. Then I went in and powered up *Might and Magic II*.

I didn't feel like working on the code anymore that day, but there were other things I could do. The party needed to grow stronger, I knew that. We were hardly strong enough for the garden beasts, and I figured eventually we'd have to face the dragons. There were probably dragons guarding the time machine, wherever it was. We needed to bulk up on the pulverized numbers of defeated foes. Rise in levels. Get powerful.

There was a dungeon beneath the palace. The entrance lay behind a door I'd thought I'd explored. Weird, I thought. These doors that sometimes have empty rooms behind them, and other times have secret gardens, dungeon entrances, throne rooms. I wondered if somehow I was already traveling in time . . .

"Next week is the last week of school, Michael," my mother said softly.

I jumped in my chair. She was standing just behind me.

"Don't you think you should stop playing that game for a while?"

"I'm busy," I mumbled.

She looked at me with her large blue eyes.

"Michael," she said finally, "listen to me."

She didn't yell. She took my hand in hers, gently, the way she used to when I was Sean's size. She looked into me with her blue eyes.

"You have a heart of gold," she whispered.

"What?"

"A heart of gold."

She was rubbing my hand gently. What the hell was this? Was Annie back with her tarot cards?

"What are you talking about, Mom?" I said carefully.

She looked at me, tears shining in her eyes. "I know, Michael."

Something caught in my throat. "I'm fine, Mom, just—"

"I know your friends have left you," Mom said. "You've lost your friends, Michael. I know that."

Suddenly a sob expanded in my chest. The devastated, zero-degree emptiness I'd felt standing before the school bathroom mirror flooded back. I jerked my hands out of hers, dug my nails into my palms.

"I know it hurts," Mom said quietly. "You can talk me. I love you. You're my son."

I shut my eyes, breathed deeply.

"You can tell me," she said. "Let it out, Michael."

"It's like everyone . . . ," I began. "They . . ."

The sound of my voice, husky with incipient weeping, frightened me.

Mom took my hand in hers again, squeezed it.

"You have a heart of gold," she said.

Don't cry, I told myself. *Do not cry.*

"Do you know what it means to have a heart of gold?" she asked.

Heart of gold. Jesus. It wasn't tarot cards. It was a line from a song. That fucking Neil Young song, she'd played it incessantly ever since my father had left. God *damn* Neil Young, I thought. I dug my nails deeper into my palm.

"Do you know what it means to have a heart of gold?" Mom asked again.

I bit my lip and shook my head.

"It means there's something in you that's good. Something you can never lose."

Then she turned and walked out of the room. As soon as she was gone, I began to cry. Tears poured silently down my face. After a while the tears fell more slowly. Then they stopped.

Then something strange happened. I felt peaceful. I wiped my nose on my sleeve. Inhaled slowly. Exhaled slowly.

A heart of gold, I thought. Not the red tangle of muscle they showed us in science class. A lasting heart. A heart made of the strong lasting stuff of the inhuman world.

•

Three minutes later, Mom came stomping back into the room. Her face had changed. Hard determination stared out of her eyes, out of the angles of her 3-D body, out of the color of her faux ruby earrings.

"I didn't finish telling you what I came in here for," she said. "I am VERY WORRIED about you, Michael. You have LOST all of your friends. If you go into this summer without any friends, what will happen to you? What will happen to you next fall, in high school? If you enter high school with no friends you could very well *never* have friends again! You could end up *completely alone*! So get off your butt! You need to fix things with these kids!"

I was taken completely by surprise by this sudden change of mood. "What about what you were just saying, Mom?"

She stared at me, hands on her hips.

"Just saying about what?" she asked.

"You know," I said, suddenly embarrassed. "About, uh, the heart of gold and stuff."

She looked at me like I was retarded.

"That's my *point*," she said. "That's what I'm *saying*. The meaning of your life is in the quality of your human relationships, Michael. My therapist says it, it says it in the Bible, everyone knows it, Michael! When we *die*, the *only* thing that matters is the *quality* of our *human relationships*."

She stared at me, searching my eyes.

"Your heart is for *meaningful relationships with other people*," she said, pronouncing each word slowly and clearly. "Now turn off this *goddamn* game and start thinking about how you can *make* these kids *like* you again."

•

I lay awake, waiting for the last Monday of middle school to dawn. I thought about what Fred and Nick had said in the bathroom. I thought about Mom's words of warning. I needed my friends back. I needed to get back in. But when you're outside, I thought, how do you get back in? Once people have stopped talking to you, how do you talk to them?

There's no way to get from the outside to the inside. Beef had proven that, and he wasn't even close to being as far outside as I was now. Beef. I'd watched Beef for a year and a half trying to find an opening into the cool kids' circle. I'd watched him trying to start a conversation with Phillip, with Fred, with Allison. They'd stare at him, stunned. Like they were watching a unicorn trying to speak, like they were watching something impossible.

And they were. You can't break into a circle. A circle is by definition unbroken. A circle goes around forever without an opening. A circle is smooth impervious circular lastingness. To get from the outside of the circle to the inside? You can't do it. You can't just walk up and ask a circle to open.

The only way to get in is to already be inside.

That's it, I thought, sitting up in bed. I had to be already inside. The code, *seven in the morning*. The code for whatever it was Phillip and Nick and Fred and Allison and Mary knew about that I didn't. That code was circular language. It was inside-speak. All I had to do was say it. You don't speak to someone *inside* the circle with *outside* language. You speak to them in their language. The only way to get from outside to inside is to already be in. I just had to show them I was already in. I just had to say the words.

But no, I thought, recalling what Nick and Fred had said about the others. "They just know the words," Fred had said. "*Seven in the morning*. They hear us say the words and they know it means something maybe, but they don't know what it means."

Okay. I had to say it like I knew what it meant. I had to internalize it, to speak their code like it was mine.

Tomorrow, I thought sleepily. Tomorrow I'll go up to Phillip and I'll just say it, in a way that showed I knew what it meant. No, not Phillip, I thought. He was *too* inside. I'll say it to Allison first. Say it like I meant it.

But what did it mean? I lay back down, sighed. Closed my eyes. Went back over the clues. *Gross*, Allison had said. Nick coughing and spitting. Seven. Morning. What did morning have to do with it? And *discover*. Yes, *discover*. No, I thought. That's the other code. The CRON code. Central Research Observational Nacelle. What did Nacelle mean? Stop it, I thought. Stay focused.

But half-sleep had left me defenseless, and all night the codes changed places in my weary brain. The impervious words went through my mind in circles.

Seven in the morning . . .

For each I inside night, discover . . .

Seven in the morning . . .

For each I inside night, discover . . .

•

The next day I watched and waited for my chance. The crucial thing was to get one of them alone. But I couldn't see how. In English class, they all sat in tight, whispering groups. Same in math. At recess, I sat by myself on the steps, thinking in codes, watching the kids playing touch football on the grass.

The field where they played was raised a bit, a little hill, really. The kids at the top moved against pure blue sky. I found that if I made a little telescope with my fingers, I could catch a kid in my sight with no trees or buildings to lend perspective. Just a head against the blue.

Could have been any size. Could have been made of anything. A flat image, with only the blue sky behind for a third dimension. With only the blue sky behind to show that the head had another side, to show it was real.

The bell jolted me from my reverie. I ran and hid behind the building, hoping to jump out and spring the code on a straggler. But the kids seemed to move in a solid mass. The building swallowed them in two seconds. I walked in alone.

By science class, the second-to-last period of the day, I was desperate. And then, with fifteen minutes left in the period, I saw Phillip raise his hand and ask to go to the bathroom. The teacher nodded, and out he went.

This is it, I thought. Now or never. I took a deep breath and raised my hand. The teacher nodded absently. I walked up to the head of the class, walked across it to the door, all the time watching the faces lose expression as I passed. I opened the door. The hallway. Dark tiles, they might have been green once. As I walked down the hall, heart beating, I hardly noticed the pale blue of the walls.

The bathroom door opened when I was three steps away. Phillip walked out, blond hair, light blue eyes, a smile dying on his lips. Stopped, because I stood right before him.

My palms sweated. My heart beat in my throat. He turned to step around me, but I cleared my throat and said, "Hey, man. I think it's about *seven in the morning*, huh?"

The vast echoing hall brought my voice back to me. It sounded nothing like I'd imagined. I'd fearfully imagined a child's squeak, a weak high voice trembling with the fear that stiffened my legs and arms and set my heart racing.

But the voice that echoed back was deep, loud, impossibly confident. As I heard it, my arms relaxed. My breath came freer. I even smiled.

Phillip looked at me uncertainly. He looked behind him, looked ahead. Licked his lips. Then he leaned toward me.

"You're talking to yourself," he whispered.

Then he was sauntering down the hall toward class.

"I'd watch that if I were you," he called back over his shoulder. "You might be going crazy."

•

I spent the last few afternoons of middle school playing *Might and Magic II*. After an hour or two I'd go out on the patio with my pencil and paper. Work on the code a little. Sometimes

Sean would come out too. He'd sit squeezing Stinky. Sometimes he'd lumber through the grass pushing his Tonkas. I'd look up, see him moving under the sky.

That sky, the sky of the May of my thirteenth year, was the most beautiful I've ever seen. The victorious sky of 1989. The magic sky.

And it really was magic. Around five in the afternoon, its color began to *move*. Suddenly, behind the outermost layer of blue, I would notice a deeper shade. The first layer gradually vanished, like the white smoke of a jet vanishes gradually. And then, half an hour later, another shade of sky, still deeper, slowly became visible through the light blue veil of the outermost layer.

The sky is moving, I'd think, looking up from my codes. The sky is traveling.

And at seven o'clock, just before Mom called us in to dinner, just before the last and deepest blue made its final departure for the stars, I'd look around.

And every blade of grass. Every twig. The tires of Sean's Tonkas. The roof of the barn. My legs, my hands—the color held them all. The way the ocean holds swimmers. The way the air holds birds.

When we die, the only thing that matters is the quality of our human relationships. It says it in the Bible. Therapists say it. I can believe it. I can easily believe that in the end, our relationships with people are what we'll remember. Personal relationships are memorable. And things you can remember matter. They matter because you can remember them. Because you can put them in a story, they matter.

But just because relationships with people fit easiest into our stories, it doesn't mean there aren't other dimensions of life. There's a warm red heart for people, true. But there's also another heart. A heart that moves through time. A heart made of the enduring stuff of mountains or stars. Or pixels. Or sky.

Phillip told me I was talking to myself, and he was right. But now I know it's not easy to talk to yourself. To *really* talk to yourself. To stand under the circular sky of your interior. It's not easy. You need a code. "For each I inside night, discover." You need a code like that to carry into you. A solid, hard bit of language, something you don't understand, something that's not yours. A ruler to measure everything that is. A fixed point. A horizon for your inner sky.

And in the same way, when we die, it isn't going to be easy to remember the part of our lives that wasn't involved with people. We need a different kind of story for that. A different way of remembering.

It's easy to grow some plants. Put soil in a pot, throw in a few seeds, water it once in a while, and up it goes. But there are other plants, plants that need more support. When gardeners want to grow some kinds of especially fragile plants, they use a stake. A pole that the shy plant slowly climbs up. Gardeners call them *climbing* plants.

Suspended. The Bard's Tale II, Ultima III, Wolfenstein, Elite, Pirates!, Might and Magic II. I stack them, one on top of the other. My shy blue life climbs slowly up. My *climbing* life.

When I die, I will remember the color of the sky.

Acknowledgments

I'd like to thank Mitzi Angel, Stan Apps, J. K. Barret, Colleen Clune, Aaron Kunin, Ben Lerner, Edward Orloff, Lauren Voss, and Will Wolfslau.